The Unknown God

The Unknown God

Sermons Responding to the New Atheists

Edited by
JOHN HUGHES

Foreword by
RICHARD CHARTRES

CASCADE *Books* • Eugene, Oregon

THE UNKNOWN GOD
Sermons Responding to the New Atheists

Cascade Books
An Imprint of Wipf and Stock Publishers
199 W. 8th Ave., Suite 3
Eugene, OR 97401

www.wipfandstock.com

ISBN 13: 978-1-4982-1431-5

Cataloging-in-Publication data:

The unknown God : sermons responding to the new atheists /
edited by John Hughes ; foreword by Richard Chartres.

xvi + 106 p. ; 23 cm. —Includes bibliographical references and
index.

ISBN 13: 978–1-61097–579-7

1. Christianity and atheism. I. Chartres, Richard, 1947–. II.
Hughes, John, 1978–. III. Title.

BR162.3 .U50 2013

Manufactured in the U.S.A.

Dedicated to the Master, Fellows, Students, and Staff
of the College of the Blessed Virgin Mary,
St John the Evangelist, and the Glorious Virgin St Radegund,
commonly called Jesus College, Cambridge

So Paul, standing in the middle of the Areopagus, said: "Men of Athens, I perceive that in every way you are very religious. For as I passed along, and observed the objects of your worship, I found also an altar with this inscription, 'To an unknown god.' What therefore you worship as unknown, this I proclaim to you."

Acts 17:22–23

Contents

Suffering and Hope

The True Revolution

Foreword

Thank God for the atheists! The reinvigoration of atheism over the last decade or so has brought the discussion of Christianity back into the public square in a way that the Church of England's "Decade of Evangelism" (the 1990s) was never able to do. Apathy, cynicism, and self-parody in the Church and wider society have increased the tendency to marginalize all religion and to exile it to the realms of private lifestyle choices to be practiced only in the company of other consenting adults.

John Hughes reminds us in his sermon that atheism has in some respects grown historically out of Reformation Christianity, and as Terry Eagleton suggests in his sermon, neo-atheism, particularly in the United States, has emerged as part of the "War on Terror" after 9/11. In other words, it is part of the human response to the mysteries of life, death, beauty, love, and ideological passion.

Healthy, opportunistic attacks by atheists on believers are as essential to the good estate of religion as an effective opposition is to any democratic government. They help preserve us from cant, from irrational fundamentalism, and from self-absorption.

Or as that wry observer of the *zeitgeist*, Woody Allen, put it rather succinctly: "To you I'm an atheist; to God, I'm the Loyal Opposition" (*Stardust Memories*, 1980).

The Rt Revd and Rt Honorable Richard Chartres
KCVO DD FSA
Bishop of London
Michaelmas 2012

Introduction

JOHN HUGHES

This little book is unlikely to persuade any atheists, new or otherwise, of the existence of God. It might, however, provide a taster for some of the more interesting theological responses to the New Atheists. If so, it might also provide some pointers toward a better understanding of the New Atheism, which is an interesting cultural and literary phenomenon in its own right, as well as perhaps suggest some more fruitful avenues of response for believers.

This book is a collection of sermons, which may well have a dusty, nineteenth-century sound to many. But sermons are in fact probably the true "front line" of theology, if not in the sense of being the coalface where new thinking begins, then at least through being the site where this theology reaches its widest dissemination, is supposed to connect with the ordinary lives of believers, and is tested against reality. Many people who would never find time to read serious works of academic theology might find time to hear or even read a sermon. Equally, for professional academics to face the task of condensing their carefully measured thinking into something that can be digested from oral delivery in between ten and twenty minutes is a valuable and demanding challenge. The constraints of the genre of a sermon are quite different from those of the lecture theatre: there is no opportunity to ask questions, and what is said, even if not spoken "authoritatively" by a duly ordained minister on behalf of the Church, still tends to command a different sort of attention from its audience.

The specific context where most of these sermons were preached is important here. Jesus College Chapel is one of the many ancient college chapels of the University of Cambridge. Despite its name and foundation by a bishop, Jesus College today is not a seminary or theology college, but a modern diverse academic community, like most Western universities, teaching a wide range of disciplines and including students of all faiths and none. The clergy and services of the Chapel are part of the Church of England, but these services will be attended not only by Christians of other traditions, but also by students, academics, and others, including many of other nationalities, who come simply to enjoy the beautiful music or to participate in a key English cultural tradition. So the preacher certainly cannot presume to be "preaching to the converted," as, unlike many churches, the presence of atheists and agnostics within the congregation can be virtually guaranteed. On the other hand, this audience and the liturgical setting within which these sermons were preached (Choral Evensong, Cranmer's combination of vespers and compline, with the addition of a substantial diet of Scripture) make for a more appropriate setting for speculative, open-ended reflections and even provocation than would be fitting at a more intensely devotional service such as the Eucharist. Likewise there is more room in this service for voices to speak who are not only not "authorized" by a church, but may even find themselves on the edges of Christianity itself.

This series of sermons, preached in the Lent term of 2011, arose out of the perception that, on the one hand, many agnostic undergraduates had acquired a new contempt for and lack of understanding of religion, due to the remarkable reach of the New Atheists' arguments, and also that many Christian students felt ill-equipped to respond intelligently to such criticisms of their faith. By this time, a number of more serious theological books had been produced in response, and it seemed worth inviting the authors of these books to preach. The two resident clergy are also represented here, as are some other authors who had been invited to be part of the series but had not been able to come. The sermons vary in length and tone, but no attempt has been made to erase the specificity of their context as *sermons*, written to be delivered at a particular time and place. Preachers were given the liberty to draw upon the readings at Evensong or not, and when they have, the details of these have been given at the start of the sermon. The collection includes a mixture of ecclesiastical traditions, with Anglican, Roman Catholic, Eastern Orthodox, and Presbyterian authors, but with one exception they are all British. This is particularly worth noting, in that much of the New Atheism debate has taken its tone from the culture wars on the other side of the Atlantic. Many of the authors here note with alarm the peculiarly violent tone of the debate, the visceral loathing of religion and desire to eliminate it from the world. They offer some suggestions as to the possible causes of this tone and plead for the importance of greater mutual understanding, as much from believers as from atheists.

Beyond this concern with tone, the authors represented here share a number of common themes in their responses to the New Atheism. We can see firstly a particular approach to history. This combines, on the one hand, a rejection of the naïve Whiggish view of history as inevitable progress from the darkness of ignorance into the light of truth (McGrath); and, on the other, a historically critical interrogation of some of the key terms used by the New Atheists. "Reason," for example, is often understood by the New Atheists according to a narrow Enlightenment notion of science, but then expanded beyond its proper limits into a view of ultimate reality ("scientism"). This metaphysical naturalism is not only itself an unfounded leap of faith that is hostile to religion; its reductionism also threatens all our ordinary ways of thinking about being human (Cunningham). In differing ways, many of the authors in this volume point toward a more sociohistorical view of human rationality, not so much an unchanging, final "view from nowhere" as a set of disciplines and practices, passed on through particular communities and developing over time (Eagleton, Jenkins, Hughes, and McGrath). Likewise they stress that scientific techniques offer one specific and powerful method of looking at and understanding reality, but not the only or final one. More imaginative, mythic, narrative, emotional, and poetic modes of understanding should not simply be dismissed as meaningless or inferior (Cornwell, Cunningham).

Just as the idea that there is one uniform thing called "Science" or "Reason" is unhelpfully crude, so the very notion of "religion" is hopelessly generalizing to deliver any serious conclusions as to whether it is "good" or "bad" for us. Such distinctions and qualifications enable the believer to recognize that there are certainly many forms of religion in the world that can be harmful and terrible, without conceding that all must be (Beattie, Fergusson, Hughes, Eagleton, Jenkins). Similarly, the New Atheist view of "faith" as the irrational invention of knowledge to fill gaps of ignorance, which is the mirror image of their view of reason, is also rejected. Faith is something more fundamental, inescapable, and existential, concerning the orientation and commitments of an entire life, rather than just an opinion about something for which we have no information. Faith is neither straightforwardly demonstrable, nor by virtue of that irrational. This alternative view of faith, presented by various authors in this volume (Eagleton, McGrath, Hughes), corresponds to the classical Christian view, so well represented by Thomas Aquinas, that God is not another "thing" within the world. If this is so, then the New Atheists may well have done believers something of a favor in killing off an idolatrous god of the gaps (Cunningham). Many of the authors therefore appeal for faith to be judged as a way of life and a complete vision of everything, rather than just a set of ideas about one particular thing in the world. In this context, the so-called problem of evil and suffering is reconceived as a practical, existential problem rather than a purely intellectual one (Cornwell, Beattie).

On the question of religion and morality, the authors of these sermons recognize that the religious have no monopoly of virtue, and indeed they note the high moral tone that characterizes the New Atheists. Yet the more historical and philosophical perspective of our contributors leads them to claim that this is not the self-evident and universal ethics of reason that some seem to believe it to be. Reason on its own is indifferent to questions of value and cannot therefore generate an ethics. Rather, our authors see the roots of the liberal ethics of the New Atheists in the Judeo-Christian tradition and argue that different views of ultimate reality (whether Christian, materialist, neo-Darwinian, or whatever) entail different ethics (Hughes, Beattie, Cunningham, Hart). Beyond this recognition of the Christian roots of liberalism, there is in a number of these sermons a critique (indebted to Marx) of the bourgeois liberalism of the New

Atheists, as fitting all too well into the logic of capitalism and being much less radical than the truly revolutionary and transformative message of hope that Christianity offers (Eagleton, Hughes, Beattie, Hart).

This collection has been titled *The Unknown God* with reference to St. Paul's debate with the philosophers at the Areopagus in Athens (Acts 17). That story shows the importance of Christians engaging sympathetically and critically with those who hold differing religious and philosophical views and who shape the patterns of thinking within a culture. St. Paul uses the altar to the unknown god as his starting point for this conversation, just as one of the key points at issue in the contemporary debate seems to be whether it is possible to have genuine knowledge of God. At the same time, part of the problem with this debate might be that the "god" who according to the atheists cannot be known to exist, is in other ways presumed by them to be all *too* knowable, an easily comprehended idol or superman whose existence can be all too readily proved or disproved like any other object or "thing" within the universe. The authors represented here speak by contrast of the God who can never finally be grasped by human reason and yet who makes himself known in and through all things, in whom we live and move and have our being.

Faith and Reason

1

Faith, Knowledge, and Terror

TERRY EAGLETON

Terry Eagleton is one of Britain's most distinguished literary critics and has held chairs in the Universities of Oxford, Manchester, and Lancaster. Raised a Roman Catholic in working-class Salford, he became active in Marxist literary circles, publishing widely on many topics. He was drawn into the New Atheism debate writing a review of The God Delusion *for the* London Review of Books *in 2006, and then delivering the Terry lectures at Yale on Faith and Fundamentalism, which became the book* Reason, Faith and Revolution. *Here he questions one of the central presuppositions of the New Atheism, arguing that "faith" is not simply opposed to atheism, because it is not just an opinion about a state of affairs, but rather "a species of love." It is not reducible to reason, but neither are they opposed: "Without reason, we perish, but reason does not go all the way down.... All knowledge takes for granted some kind of faith." Eagleton then offers some brief reflections on the historical situation that has given birth to the New Atheism, especially 9/11 and the War on Terror.*

—JH

One reason why a dialogue between faith and atheism is so hard is that they are not really the same kind of thing. Things that are the opposites of each other—say, capitalism and socialism, or militarism and pacifism—can argue with each other easily enough. They have enough in common precisely as opposites to make this possible. But this only seems to be true in the case of atheism and religious faith. It is not exactly that we have here what the philosophers would call a category mistake, as though putting faith and atheism on the same level were as ridiculous as trying to compare one's left foot with the Mona Lisa. Even so, the idea that faith and atheism can confront each other as candidates for dialogue is partly an illusion of our grammar, as Wittgenstein might have put it. Our grammar makes them sound like the same kind of thing, as it makes sexual jealousy and the pancreas sound like the same kind of thing. But in fact they are not. This is one reason why atheists and believers seem constantly to be talking past each other. Their conversations have the slightly surreal quality of a quarrel over veal escalope between a food scientist and a *bon viveur*.

Take the difference between being in love with someone and not being in love with them. To be in love is a bond, a commitment, a project, an experience, an act of self-giving. It is something one does, not just a condition one happens to be in like having chicken pox or a fiver in the bank. Not being in love with someone, by contrast, is not the opposite sort of experience or commitment. It is not an experience or commitment at all. There is no such thing as the experience of not being in love with Donald Rumsfeld, any more than there is such a thing as the experience of not having freckles or purple-dyed hair, or not being Britney Spears. You can be decidedly not in love with someone, but not passionately so. (Wittgenstein, incidentally, thought that many things we considered to be experiences were actually not. Promising, expecting, and intending, for example. He also once observed that love was not a feeling. This may be hard for the readers of Catherine Cookson to understand, but not for readers of the New Testament.)

The problem is that atheism is not a faith but a belief. You can, of course, hold intensely atheistic convictions, like Richard Dawkins and other such old-fashioned nineteenth-century rationalists, rather than simply holding the cool intellectual opinion that there is no God. But this is not enough to turn belief into faith. You can be passionately convinced that the Queen is a North Korean spy, but this is still a question of belief even though you would stake your life on it. The difference between faith and belief is not one of degrees of intensity. You can have a moderate faith, just as you can have a full-blooded belief. The historian A. J. P. Taylor once told a committee interviewing him for an Oxford fellowship that he had extreme political views, but held them moderately.

The opposite of atheism is not faith, but believing in the existence of God. These two opinions are certainly the same kind of thing. They are, so to speak, on all fours with one another. But believing in the existence of God is not the same thing as having faith in him. The devils are said to do the former, but they do not do the latter. Abraham had faith in God, but given his cultural circumstances he could scarcely have conceived of his nonexistence. Having faith in one's children is not the same as believing in their existence, though the former presupposes the latter. Faith (not just religious faith) is a species of love, as Kierkegaard recognized. And though love entails beliefs, it is not reducible to them.

Neither is it reducible to reason, though it entails that as well. A durable love has to be a reasonable one. It does not make sense to declare that you love Donald Trump if you are able to give absolutely no reasons why you do. Even so, someone else could agree with your reasons yet not be in love with him. Without reason, we perish, but reason does not go all the way down. To suppose that it does is one of the errors of the rationalists. Another such mistake is to assume that reason and faith are opposites. Almost all rationalists, in short, are fideists, if non-believing fideists. But there is nothing irrational about having faith in one's best friend. It may not always be warranted, but that's a different matter.

I said just now that having faith in one's children presupposes believing in their existence, but the relationship between the two is actually closer than that makes it sound. Knowing a person is not like knowing a lawnmower. As one comes to know a person better, he or she develops the trust and affection to open up to you and take the risk of revealing themselves for what they are, confident in the faith that you will not thereby reject them. This tends not to be the case with lawnmowers, unless I've had the ill luck to encounter exceptionally shy ones. This is one of several senses in which love and knowledge, or faith and knowledge, are not at loggerheads. There is a sense in which only by having faith in you can I know you as you really are—know you in a way fuller than I can ever know a possum or a potato. All knowledge takes for granted some kind of faith. Not even Richard Dawkins would bother to stroll into the laboratory if he was as convinced as Arthur Schopenhauer that there was simply no point to human rationality.

Of course, I believe in your existence in the sense that I believe in the existence of a fire hydrant or an aspen tree. But this purely notional knowledge, as Newman might have put it, will not do anything for either me or the fire hydrant (though Thomas Aquinas would have demurred on the latter point). It is as dysfunctional in my existence as knowing that you cannot fly from the capital of Croatia to the capital of Slovenia, a piece of knowledge around which for some curious reason my life does not seem to turn.

Not enough has been made of the connection between the New Atheism and the so-called War on Terror. Why is it that in a supposedly post-metaphysical, post-theological, postmodern age, God is suddenly back on the agenda, just when he was preparing to take a much-deserved retirement in bitter regret that he had ever created the slightest particle of matter? There are all kinds of reasons for this irony, but one might do worse than mention 9/11. The West now finds itself confronted by a particularly ugly species of religious fundamentalism at just the moment when it has itself, so to speak, spiritually disarmed, living as it does by an unholy melange of pragmatism, cultural relativism, instrumental reason, anti-foundationalism, and the death of grand narratives. This kind of stuff is hardly enough to face down those who cling to absolute truths and rock-solid foundations.

It is not entirely surprising, then, though it is certainly profoundly ironic, that just at the point where a postmodern era had supposedly abandoned all belief in the grand narratives of Reason, Science, Progress, and Enlightenment, a crude, off-the-peg, reach-me-down version of them known as neo-atheism has been suddenly revived. Europe, the cradle of civility and rationality, once more gazes anxiously out at a dark-skinned world of bigotry and fanaticism. The truth is that there are indeed fanatics intent on blowing off the heads of the innocent in the name of God, but you do not have to look to Damascus or Islamabad to find them. Quite a lot of them can be found in the cabins of Montana or small-town Alabama. Barbarism and civilization are not to be so easily distinguished. Which, exactly, was the war on Iraq?

There is a smack of both Western triumphalism and cultural supremacism about quite a lot of the New Atheism. It is by no means a politically innocent enterprise. It is a Pelagian tale about humanity—a just-so story for which we in the West are growing steadily nicer and nicer, more and more civilized and humane, and would no doubt sail triumphantly ahead into some rationalist utopia were it not for the stubborn remnants of an outmoded religiosity. Like all such hubristic denial of the frailty and flawedness of humanity, it is likely to come a cropper. In fact, it has already done so. It is precisely this brand of Western triumphalism, of which some of the New Atheism is, so to speak, the intellectual wing, that in its political rather than intellectual form has wreaked such havoc over the decades in the Muslim world. And it is partly in reaction to that havoc and humiliation that the heads of the innocent are now being blown off.

2

The Ethics of Being Reasonable

DAVID FERGUSSON

David Fergusson is Professor of Divinity and Principal of New College, Edinburgh, and a minister in the Presbyterian Church of Scotland. He has written on the relationship between the Church, the State, and Civil Society and published Faith and Its Critics: A Conversation *in 2009. Fergusson's interest in public life is reflected here in his observations about the tone of public debate, in particular in the House of Commons and on Internet blogs. He notes the violent hostility on both sides of the New Atheism debate and urges that a respectful attention to the views of others is a key factor in a civilized society. For Christians this should go even further: if we are to preach a message of peace, charity, and humility, then this should be reflected in the form as well as the content of what we say. While it is incumbent upon all Christians to give an account of the faith that we have, yet perhaps we can see even the New Atheists as a providential gift to correct and renew the faith of the Church, which must be proclaimed afresh in every generation.*

—JH

Prime Minister's question time now takes place each Wednesday. It is covered on TV and we are treated to the highlights on the evening news and in the parliamentary sketches of the broadsheets the following day. By most standards, the behavior is pretty awful. Last week, it looked even worse when Sky News attempted to lip-read the reactions of people goading the party leaders. I'm not sure if this is allowed under the broadcasting rules—it certainly stretched them—but it revealed a little more of the baiting, jeering, abusing, and general pantomime behavior.

It is argued that robust debate and exchanges are necessary in a democracy. Our leaders need to be held to account and challenged, rather than treated with undue deference. Having read arguments to that effect, I'm not wholly convinced. In most sectors of our society, that sort of conduct in the workplace would lead very quickly to formal complaints of intimidation and inappropriate behavior. Schoolchildren are never permitted to comport themselves in that way. If you had spoken to your mother in those tones, you might have been sent to bed without your dinner. In twenty-five years of university teaching, I can only recall once having been heckled by a student in a lecture, and he at least had the excuse of being drunk. Plenty have fallen asleep or absented themselves—in this respect, the lecture theatre resembles not the Commons, but the Lords. The Commons seems to break many of the rules of dignity and respect that govern other workplaces, and I wonder whether this serves political argument very well. In case you think I am taking the high moral ground, however, it may be worth adding that the Scottish Parliament now seems to be moving in the same direction. After a good deal of pious rhetoric about a new style of politics, more consensual debate, and cross-party cooperation, First Minister's question time is beginning to resemble an etiolated version of Westminster.

Are there other places where people are able to be disgracefully rude about their fellow citizens in public? Well, maybe there are more than we think. Our football grounds are now all-seater stadiums, but the behavior isn't all that much better. You can hurl abuse at opposing players and fans that could easily get you arrested if spoken on the street. The culture of blogging provides opportunities for rapid responses, caustic reaction and vitriolic comment, usually under the cloak of electronic anonymity. To create an effect, it helps if you can occupy an extreme position, shout loudly, or ridicule your opponent.

Much of the recent discussion on religion reflects this new context for public debate. We've had blogs and gladiatorial debates in which faith is mocked variously as absurd, quaint, outmoded, dangerous, violent, and corrupting of the young—it's not clear how all of these claims can be true simultaneously, but it hasn't stopped some of the critics. Web sites, correspondence columns, and public discussions have all been devoted to the New Atheism. London buses have run campaigns sponsored by humanists. "There is probably no God. Now stop worrying and enjoy your life." A service of lessons and carols for the ungodly is held each Christmas at which Richard Dawkins now reads from some of his own works—it seems that these have had some sort of canonical status now conferred upon them. All this makes for good theatre, and it enlivens discussion in common rooms, dinner parties, and pubs. But does it offer us heat rather than light? Is the noise–signal ratio so poor that we fail to pick up the content of the message rather than the shrill forms in which it is expressed? It's interesting that some feminist writers have complained about the way in which the debate has become polarized. One critic has suggested that there is something a little comic about this perennial stag-fight between men with big ideas.

Of course, the traffic is two-way. Critics of religion have their intemperate and discourteous exponents, but so too do its defenders. Richard Dawkins receives an ugly postbag of comments from those who would criticize him. The tone is often nasty, personal, and vindictive. The expression "*odium theologicum*" was originally coined to describe the odious behavior not of scientists or humanists but of Christian theologians in their behavior to one another. At the time of the Enlightenment, it was the skeptic David Hume who pleaded for courtesy, conversation, good manners, and calm debate amongst people of differing persuasions, and he sought to practice this with a light touch. Having emerged from a history of religious violence, he knew where it could lead. So it cuts both ways, and we need to recognize that faith has been practiced and defended in ways that are absurd, unfair, and malicious.

In the seventeenth century, defenders of religious toleration like John Milton believed that the truth could only emerge if there was a peaceful public space in which citizens could disagree with one another without recourse to coercion or civil war. This was not borne of indifference or a view that anything went—only through conversation and an honest exchange of opinion could greater wisdom be found.

I leave three brief observations with you about our current situation. First, it is incumbent upon people of faith to offer some account of what they do and think. In the New Testament, the letter of Peter makes this apparent: "Give a reasoned defense to those who would challenge you" (1 Pet 3:15). This was written at a time of persecution and hostility toward small Christian groups in the Graeco-Roman world, but it remains a responsibility wherever there are differences and a plurality of worldviews. No doubt this takes many forms but it is an obligation of one's convictions. Second, we are charged in another epistle to correct our opponents "with gentleness and courtesy" (2 Tim 2:25)—a text too often ignored or discarded. The reason for this is quite simple. The Christian gospel is about the love and generosity of God to the most undeserving, especially ourselves. If so, then its expression ought to match its content. It seeks friendship and maintains respect even amidst disagreement and divergence—admittedly, that's not always easy since we tend naturally to seek out the company of those who are like us and think as we do. But the truth is not promoted by demonizing our opponents.

Finally, the encounter with criticism of religion may also enrich faith. Faith is never static or immutable but changes and adapts across history, and that is true of our own pilgrimages and life-histories. How we understand and express our faith now is likely to differ ten or twenty years on. The history of the Church includes belief commitments that many of us would now regard as implausible or uncharitable. The doctrine of predestination taught by Augustine, Aquinas, and Calvin is seldom expounded by theologians today. The belief that infants who die unbaptized go to hell or even limbo has always been a source of unease. What we believe about Adam, Eve, and the serpent has changed in the last four hundred years. I had a Sunday school teacher who expounded to us the thesis that the extinction of dinosaurs was on account of their being too large to enter Noah's ark. Even as children, we sensed that there was something a bit odd about that hypothesis.

Why did God create atheists? It's a whimsical question that the Chief Rabbi, Jonathan Sacks, has posed on several occasions. His answer is that they prevent us from believing the wrong things or investing too much in matters of secondary importance. That is good advice. The encounter with criticism and doubt affords an opportunity for deeper reflection, self-criticism and an advance in wisdom. But that's unlikely to be achieved by the "ya-boo" behavior of Prime Minister's question time. Better a little conversation, some honest exchange and quiet deliberation, than point scoring and public acclaim. As Jesus said, blessed are the meek, for they shall inherit the earth.

Darwin and Dawkins

3

Popular Science
and Science Fiction
TIMOTHY JENKINS

Timothy Jenkins is Assistant Director of Research in the Study of Religion in the Faculty of Divinity at Cambridge University and fellow of Jesus College. He is a priest of the Church of England and also a social anthropologist and author of Religion in English Everyday Life. *In this sermon he provides an analysis of the genre of Richard Dawkins'* The God Delusion. *He argues that the tone is that of an autodidact rather than the methodology of genuine scientific research. Dawkins' work belongs more to a particular genre of the popularization of science, through bringing together a popular account of the present situation of "religion" and "science." The polemic against religion involves an overly simplistic account of ethical behavior, as if the disappearance of religion would remove moral evils and scientific reason could simply generate its own ethics. More significantly, Dawkins offers a popularization of Darwinism in terms that exclude the possibility of social rationality as anything other than epiphenomenal. Yet, as Jenkins argues, such a position excludes the very practices of science itself.*

—JH

How best to characterize the effect of reading Dawkins' *The God Delusion*? He leaves a strong and by no means unpleasant taste in the mouth, but of what does it remind one? Listening to a critic review the book on the radio, she said it was like sitting at a table in the pub with a man who is determined to argue, no matter how much you agree with him. That I think is right; Dawkins' essential characteristic is that he sounds like an *autodidact*—a man of considerable intelligence and wide reading, but insufficiently acquainted with the disciplines and histories that lie behind what he has read. He simply believes that the books that he agrees with are true, and the books he disagrees with wrong. This is a recurrent problem with adult learners in a university context: they know how to read new material and put it to work for their own ends, but cannot learn or relearn the ability to be changed by what they read. They are already shaped and so, from another perspective, unteachable. Dawkins is not looking for instruction, but wishes to impart what he has read, to one particular end, which may be summed up as "don't get me started on religion . . ."—meaning quite the opposite.

Is this a fair characterization? Certainly, he covers a lot of ground: we are given samples of reading encompassing aspects of metaphysics, moral philosophy, biology, psychology, sociology, anthropology, history, the Bible, contemporary Islam, American evangelicalism and the Moral Majority, and European Catholicism. This is not an exhaustive list. But more important is the way he handles these eclectic materials. By "autodidact" I mean to point to the following. Although he claims to be a scientist (as, indeed, in real life he has been), there is no evidence of a scientific approach nor of scientific habits of mind. There is simply a display of knowledge, of examples that serve to illustrate the argument, and no sense of the materials developing an argument. The knowledge he invokes is therefore inert rather than alive. In accordance with this approach, he cites writers he agrees with as authorities, and likewise derides authors with whom he disagrees; there is no notion of evaluating evidence—although we are incited to refer to evidence rather than opinion, that is not the practice of the author. Matching this, he fails to give any sense that the various disciplines he invokes have their own histories of debate and discovery of provisional findings, and that each case study provides specific answers to specific questions, and that it is important to know what the questions were to which these are the answers. Instead, we are given an accumulation of facts, which are held to be self-evident and universal in their application. Moreover, in the course of an argument, Dawkins moves to and fro in terms of scale between the particular and the universal; he can start from a small-scale example and move to a broad assertion, which he will then further illustrate with examples drawn from other contexts. He lacks any constructed "middle distance," in which the general and the specific (which may well themselves be less large and less small respectively than the universal and the particular) are held together in certain amalgams and relations. Lastly, because he lacks any concept of context or necessary connection, we are never offered the thorough coverage of any question, with breaking down a case into simpler elements and building up the patterns of relations; rather, we are given the tracing of single elements (often a word) through different frames and contexts. In a sentence, this is not Baconian science, but only a simulacrum of it.

The effect is paradoxical, because while on the surface we are offered a positivist account of facts, to be opposed to human history and culture, at a deeper level we are caught up in a thoroughly cultural, historical product, a discourse on "science" and "religion." One should be pretty cautious in trying to characterize "science," not least because the various sciences do not have much in common. But one might suggest that at least some work through a dialectic of materialized theories (in equipment) and theorized materials, giving rise to a series of successive controlled approximations. The fascination and power of scientific thinking lies in the specificity of the understanding it produces in each case, including an awareness of the limits of its application. Therein too lie its disappointments: it cannot readily generate universals. Even a "theory of everything" is in practice an equation that claims to relate four other equations. Yet Dawkins' account lacks any insight into the motivations and values of scientific research, and instead develops a rhetoric that draws upon the prestige and interest of the sciences without paying attention to their practices. In doing so, he shares in the techniques and aims of a whole range of scientists who write for a popular audience and of writers who attempt to explain recent scientific advances to the same audience, who tend to create what we may call cosmologies and theodicies, explanations of the nature of the world and evaluations of its possible futures, that not only draw upon the prestige of the sciences but also utilize a concept of "Science" as a cornerstone of these accounts.

I shall return to this topic below, for locating the genre of Dawkins' book is a key to understanding its merits.

Before doing so, let me point out that the tension between the claims to factuality and the essentially humanistic discourse that is developed beneath their protection is expressed in the text in a lack of focus, a certain slippage between topics, and in uncertainties, even vulgarities, of style. This is worth pointing out because it is missed by many readers; take this comment from the back cover, by Philip Pullman (a children's writer): "*The God Delusion* is written with all the clarity and elegance of which Dawkins is a master. It is so well written, in fact..." Or this one, from the same place, by Steven Pinker (a popularizer of science): "... Richard Dawkins, one of the best non-fiction writers alive today, has assembled his thoughts on religion into a characteristically elegant book." Pullman and Pinker are mistaken; the book is neither well written nor elegant—if elegance stands in opposition to caprice. Dawkins has a limited imaginative grasp of the authors he agrees with, and less of those he disagrees with, but he also writes badly, with abrupt changes in register and the rather clumsy insertion of jokes; worse, he tells you what to think rather than showing you how to make judgements—hence the use of adjectives and adverbs to prejudice the reader—and he cannot choose in what genre to write, turning to polemic, testimony, journalism, and popularizing science in turn. When his critics praise the elegance of his writing, they mean nothing more than that they agree with his project (which is a perfectly proper thing to do), so let us try in turn to understand Dawkins' thesis.

As well as supporters, Dawkins has his detractors. However, attempts to refute one aspect or another of the work cannot offer a successful way to understanding Dawkins' thesis. Eagleton's ironic review titled "Lunging,

Flailing, Mispunching" (*LRB* 19/10/2006), while something of a master class pointing out some of the subtleties of classical theological readings and contemporary Christian defenses, would not convince anyone sympathetic to Dawkins' approach; indeed, it would simply offer confirmatory evidence. Here is a statement on behalf of a religious system, determined to win on its own terms—even if the system is represented by a fellow traveler rather than a paid-up party member. Similarly, discussion by a cognitive psychologist as to whether Dawkins has fully grasped the thesis that "religion is a by-product of the workings of normal, cognitive mechanisms . . . that have evolved for reasons unrelated to religion *per se*"[1] is beside the point. We should consider the positive case that Dawkins proposes, for that is what moves his sympathetic readers, and this case I believe is organized through two strands of argument.

The first strand is a polemic against religion, often cast in terms that are reminiscent of Nietzsche, who is not, however, mentioned in the index. In the unlikely event of his not having read him, Dawkins might enjoy him, for they share a common objective, which is to make the world a better place by freeing man from his debilitating illusions, religion among them. There is much to applaud and enjoy in these polemical sections, although the reader picks and chooses according to taste—Eagleton, for example, is quite content to allow Dawkins to gnaw on the neocons, the Taliban, and Texan Fundamentalists. Dawkins' problems in this strand lie in two connected issues. On the one hand, even if he were right, and religion were in large part responsible for the world's ills, he has not got much to set up against it, for a rational scientific understanding seems a weak force to set up against the hardwired motivations and commitments expressed in religion: understanding, like regret, will be

1. Markusson, "Review of *The God Delusion*."

too little and too late. On the other hand, his is not a plausible thesis: even were it possible to conjure away religion, there is enough evidence that bad things would continue to occur unabated, quite as much as good. Dawkins works hard to show that good does not depend upon God and, somewhat obsessively, that the bad of Stalin and Hitler does not depend upon their atheism. Yet at another level, it is naïve to link reason, especially in its scientific or technical forms, to ethical behavior, whether or not you see religion as being capable of being more than an ideological expression of error. Goods and ills emerge in this world in a far more complex, ambiguous, and interconnected manner than Dawkins can account for, and this absence underlies the sense one gains in reading of a certain lack of moral imagination. (As a remark to the side, it would be possible to construe religions as quite small-scale collective practices that serve both their practitioners and others to live and respond creatively—though not necessarily "correctly" from a perspective informed by natural science—in such a complex, ambiguous, and mixed world. But that is not a line to be developed here.)

Despite these limits (which are remarked with much greater felicity by Eagleton), a great part of Dawkins' appeal to his readers lies in this account he offers of the world and of the place of men and women in such a world: he offers a theodicy, an account of good and evil, and of man's well-being and woe. His account bears a number of characteristic marks: it claims a scientific status, drawing upon scientific vocabulary; it looks to education as the means of enlightenment and of spreading the truth; and it is "democratic," in the sense of holding knowledge to be open to and available to all. In all these respects, Dawkins' theory resembles accounts of the world that he would—and does—strongly reject, in particular, mesmerism, spiritualism, spiritual healing, and phrenology. These in their time were also widely held theodicies that built upon an appreciation of contemporary science, in the instance, popular apprehensions of Newtonianism and of the discovery of electricity (the best account I know of these movements is Logie Barrow's *Independent Spirits* [1986]). The reason that this comparison offers something more than a superficial resemblance is that the second strand of Dawkins' account—its heart—relies upon an apprehension of Darwinism.

In Dawkins' perspective, Darwinism consists in individual units seeking their own self-interest (defined as self-replication), controlled by competition. This mechanism is required to explain all aspects of human life, including the social: it is the principle of intelligibility of human behavior. It is important to note that Dawkins proposes a series of Darwinian accounts at different scales—the gene, the individual, the meme—that purposely exclude the social group: his intention is to derive various kinds of collective or social behavior, including religious and moral behavior, as by-products of these forms subject to selection. The notion of memes—units of cultural inheritance—is clearly the most relevant to the discussion of religion and morality, and yet is the least clearly defined as to how they exist and their means of transmission. For Dawkins, memes allow that there be a pool of cultural options, on the analogy of a gene pool, so that competition may drive down some forms and elevate others. We might think of such forms being transmitted by social institutions, but the issue for Dawkins is one of scale: his examples include limericks, knots, stitches, origami patterns, and useful tricks in carpentry and pottery. He is therefore consistent in excluding social behavior from any kind of explanatory function. Once one places intelligibility in the effects of competition between individual units (at whatever scale), collective phenomena must be secondary and explicable in terms reducible to the basic mechanism, and may be construed in this way as error. For this reason, Dawkins expends a good deal of energy upon the traditional topics of duty and compassion—or altruism, in its biological guise—in which individuals appear to make claims on others that trump those others' self-interestedness. In these arguments, the focus is the contrast between scientific explanations that emerge from competition between individual forms, on the one hand, and social explanations that misleadingly claim to substitute for them, on the other. So (to offer my own example), biological reproduction and genetics would be concerned with facts, while (anthropological) notions of kinship would be based upon illusion; Dawkins distinguishes in this sort of case between factual and nonfactual beliefs. There is a difficulty, however, with this kind of contrast; it may be well and good when the purpose is to distinguish between the positive truths of science and the illusions of religion and morality, but the shears of relevance cut too far, for scientific rationality is also a collective, social institution, just as much as are the rejected forms of social life. Just as in the first strand, where it is naïve to imagine good and bad effects are sufficiently distinct natural kinds that are generated by truthful and illusory forms respectively, to be readily distinguished and separated, so in this instance the proffered basis of intelligibility does not allow us to choose unambiguously between distinct forms of life. Too much indeed is conceded by recourse to a purely Darwinian account; it is not clear, if we were truly Darwinian, what could be the communicable basis of scientific truth. If we were Darwinian without remainder, we could not truly know it.

The limitations are not, of course, crucial, any more than those of the polemic against religion: they are simply the price to be paid in this kind of writing, with its mix of appeals to immediate experience, premature generalizations, and imponderable universals. Beneath the appeal to Science, embodied in the genius of Darwin, we have a deliberate, skillful, and rhetorical presentation of a theodicy, to be sold in the marketplace of such ideas, with the aim of persuading and even converting hearers to a secular salvation. One might notice in this regard Dawkins' concessions to the practice of using appearances, even when they go against the truth, to support a cause (for example, pages 115 and 239).

The success of the book may then be explained by its belonging to a tradition, going back nearly two hundred years, of deploying simultaneously popular accounts of the Christian religion together with popular accounts of the latest scientific discoveries in order to offer some kind of moral picture of the present. The two major forms of authoritative truth available to us are brought into some kind of a relationship to explain who we are and where we are going and what our potential might be. The relationship will include aspects of opposition and of cooperation between the two forms of authority (Dawkins, like Nietzsche, admires Jesus as an ethical innovator and cannot stand Paul). Dawkins therefore fits somewhere in a spectrum that includes not only spiritualism and astrology, but also Fundamentalism and the New Age, fantasy literature, science fiction, and popular science, as well as a great deal more. A good proportion of what is currently published and that sells well belongs to this kind of writing. To have built a popular Darwinianism, comparable to the popular Newtonianism of the nineteenth century, is a remarkable achievement, although the tribute may not be acceptable to the author. And although it claims to be a true account, that motif is part of the genre, as are the various stylistic and argumentative features we noted at the outset.

There is one other feature to be considered that sets Dawkins out from his fellow authors, and that is the degree to which he has been endorsed by the British scientific establishment. The names praising Dawkins' work on the back cover are exactly the kind one would expect, if you accept my argument: they are drawn from fantasy literature, popular science writing, experimental popular music, and conjuring. But Dawkins is also a Professor at the University of Oxford and, more particularly, a Fellow of the Royal Society. What are we to make of that? Dawkins' Chair is in the Public Understanding of Science, and the tradition of academic freedom, including allowing appointees to develop their post as they see fit, is a long-standing one in British universities. The Royal Society, however, has a scrupulous system of scrutiny before election, so it is legitimate to ask whether this style of thought and expression is representative of what is acknowledged to be excellent by the best British scientists and, if so, should it be a matter for discussion that they cannot tell Stork from Butter? The answer will lie somewhere in the gap between the practice of scientists and the notion of "the public understanding of science," and the difficulties of conveying the significance of scientific work to the public mind, including establishing its claims upon the public purse. We might remark that the tone and style Dawkins adopts are reminiscent of a good many of the contemporary writings of eminent scientists addressing a wider public; although he is more successful than they, he gives a clue to quite an interesting problem—as how to communicate the discoveries of scientific research without recourse to a Metaphysics of Science—that haunts the profession. This may connect in turn with the practical problem of recruitment of students to study the sciences that confronts British universities: if this is the face that laboratory science presents to intelligent young people, some of the best may be confused and even put off. There may therefore be an issue here, if not of the self-understanding of the scientific establishment, of its self-presentation.

This issue is not novel. It is at least worth comparing the excitement raised around Dawkins' work to that connected with an earlier debate from the 1960s around C. P. Snow's *The Two Cultures*, which focused upon the relationship of the sciences to the arts and humanities. The major protagonists were Snow, a scientist who, after a brief laboratory life, had become a public figure, a writer and an administrator, and F. R. Leavis, an academic concerned with the detailed practices of education and moral formation. Many of the same issues (usefully summarized in the introduction to a reprint of Snow's essay by Stefan Collini) come up in one guise or another, though it is notable that Dawkins need take no account of literature as an academic project. Now the targets are rather the last resistances of the social scientists. But the forms of the debate, and the intellectual problems they pose, persist over a longer timescale, and are in some sense definitive of our time.

4

Dawkins the Neanderthal and Darwin's Pious Idea

CONOR CUNNINGHAM

Conor Cunningham is Assistant Director of the Centre for Theology and Philosophy and a lecturer in Theology and Religious Studies at Nottingham University. He is the author of The Genealogy of Nihilism *and* Darwin's Pious Idea *and presented the BBC2 documentary* Did Darwin Kill God? *In this sermon he argues that "ultra-Darwinism" or "Darwinian fundamentalism" represents an extreme reductionist materialism, beyond that of Darwin himself, or any genuinely scientific position. Its functionalism operates like an acid destroying not only religion, but just about all the meaningfulness of ordinary life, so that we can no longer speak of people, freedom, goodness, thoughts, or even truth itself. For this sort of extreme naturalism, all these appearances are just deceptions covering the will to survive. Cunningham compares this*

to the Christian heresies of Gnosticism and Zwinglian views
of the Eucharist, arguing that ironically such a position ends
up by destroying even the ideas of matter and evolution.

—JH

The late Stephen J. Gould coined the term "ultra-Darwinism" for those who used Darwin's theory of evolution as a universal theory—in other words, as a First Philosophy, as metaphysics. He wisely saw this to be a very dangerous endeavor. One such ultra-Darwinist is Daniel Dennett, who likens Darwin's theory to a dangerous idea. He does this because he argues that it is analogous to universal acid.

Darwin's theory, a theory born in the lecture hall, rips off the architrave, spills out onto the corridors of the academy, and absorbs all other disciplines, especially the humanities. I argue that any such effort is a self-defeating ideology, but more than that it is, in effect, anti-evolutionary, for the simple reason that it rejects the fruits of evolution, insofar as it deems them less than worthy, or as wholly opposite, and opposed, to what we might think of as spiritual.

The Neanderthal will be our guiding figure here. A Neanderthal is a form of hominoid, one that was less evolved than *Homo sapiens* (at least in terms of cognitive ability). The name Neanderthal derives from the seventeenth-century theologian Joachim Neander, who was removed from his theological teaching position for refusing to take Holy Communion. (The term *Homo neanderthalensis* was coined by William King in 1863. He was a former student of Charles Lyell and was a professor of geology at Queen's College in Galway). Neander used to take walks in a local valley, which became known as the Neander Valley, and it was there that fossils were subsequently discovered. There is something rather telling about this coincidence, for, as we shall see, what is in keeping with all Gnostic paganism (most prominent in secular materialism) is an analogous refusal that material elements can give rise to real blood and a true body, or real objects. Under this logic, the elements remain bread and wine, or mere elements, but more importantly, the bread and wine are denied their own validity, so to speak, as they too are reduced or rendered epiphenomenal, mere shadows cast by the "solidity" of matter (whatever that may be). In this way, to be a Neanderthal is precisely to refuse the fruits of evolution, that is, it is to deny all height because it begins from the ground.

Ultra-Darwinists, otherwise here known as "Darwinian fundamentalists," in following the pattern of the Neanderthal, propagate what we might call a Zwinglian metaphysics—no offense to Zwingli, of course! (It may be wise to point out that the term "Darwinian fundamentalist," as with "ultra-Darwinist," was coined by an atheist scientist—in this case, Richard Lewontin—and therefore is not the invention of those religious opponents of Darwin who, no doubt, bear the obligatory froth at the edge of their mouth.)

In a similar fashion, materialists (at least crude ones, who, to be honest, tend to stack the galleries) do the same, insofar as one of their main rhetorical moves is to remind us in as severe a fashion as can be mustered that we are, yes, material—their extended fingers pointing triumphantly to our organs, to our metabolic systems, and, more often than not, to our brains, doing so with a palpable sense of "aha"! Thus we stand accused. At least that is how their story goes. Once more, the pre-Darwinian, not to say theological, heterodoxy of such logic is evident.

As the Jewish thinker Hans Jonas rightly says, "In the hue and cry over the indignity done to man's metaphysical status in the doctrine of his animal descent, it was overlooked that by the same token some dignity had been restored to the realm of life as a whole. If man was the relative of animals, then animals were the relatives of man and in degrees bearers of that inwardness of which man, the most advanced of their kin, is conscious in himself."[1] But of course, for the theologian (and we are sure many others), this all seems to be stuff and nonsense. After all, according to Christianity, a beaten, mutilated, and executed first-century Palestinian Jew, left hanging from a tree outside the city amongst all its refuse, is God incarnate. And of course, before the execution, the Logos passed through the birth canal, to be born amidst the sweat, blood, and excrement of mammalian birth. He walked amongst us, defecating, eating food, sweating just like the rest of us. And that's just Christian orthodoxy. Moreover, any such accusation of being "merely material" is the equivalent of saying a theoretical physicist is made from carbon, and so being done with their thought.

I read recently in the newspaper that Richard Dawkins has funded a children's summer camp, one that will encourage atheism, or what Dawkins would probably spin as "open-mindednesses." The problem being, as we shall see, that most atheist philosophy denies the existence of mind; open-mindedness is, therefore, an oxymoron, for it is so open, it has fallen out altogether. The old campfire song "Kumbaya" is to be replaced with John Lennon's secular hymn "Imagine." In that song we are asked to imagine a world without religion—"it's easy if you try, no hell below us, above us only sky," and so on. If we would only embrace this rational account of the world, then most of our

1. Jonas, *Phenomenon of Life*, 57.

problems would vanish, all the religious superstition and mumbo jumbo, all that theological guff. And in its place, we would behold a pristine nature, overflowing with self-evident sensibleness. Not at all, quite the reverse! Indeed, it is here that we can locate the cultural confusion that has bedeviled the debate between science and religion, between the natural and the supernatural. For we have, it seems, articulated this debate in a wholly question-begging manner, and I must say that both sides are guilty of the same crime. On the one hand, we have theologians and religious people speaking about their faith in a manner that leads them to be guilty of what I would term "anonymous atheism," to corrupt a phrase of Karl Rahner. They have bought into the idea that the supernatural is something discontinuous or unrelated to the natural; it is, in short, something extra, even if, to them, it is something extra special. This is reminiscent of Descartes' division of reality into mind and extended matter, a division that arguably accommodates the eradication of the former and the veneration of the latter—in other words, the division allows for the eradication of mind. Doing so because it provides a certain credulity to the just-so story named "materialism," with its various foundational myths—nay, fictions—especially something called "matter," or the merely material, which is on a par with the unicorn, and at least the former is a mental composition of actual entities. But of course, Hegel had already pointed to the vacuous nature of materialism, arguing that the word *matter* remains an ideal unless you pick out something material, but for there to be *something* material, materialism cannot be true. As Peter van Inwagen writes, "One of the tasks that confronts the materialist is this: they have to find a home for the referents of the terms of ordinary speech within a world that is entirely material—or else deny the existence of those referents altogether." Or as G. K.

Chesterton put it, "there is no such thing as a thing."[2] In this way, materialism appears to preclude identity.

Religious people have bought into the idea that faith is something of a lifestyle choice, like marathon running or Pilates (or mere individual salvation, understood as a "ticket" that gets us somewhere else, namely, heaven—a bit like that *very special* holiday we have always been saving for). And here the New Atheist is in complete agreement: religion is indeed something extra. The supernatural is therefore over and above the purely natural (*natura pura*), but for them, in the name of economy—Ockham's razor, if you will—we can just ignore it, setting it adrift, to the point where it becomes irrelevant. For we can indeed imagine its absence, and thus can get along without it very well, thank you very much; why not, it doesn't seem to do very much.

The banishment of God, something enabled by the strict opposition of the natural and the supernatural, has come at an enormous cost. We have ended up in a world, a supposedly natural world, that is devoid of that which we presume to be natural: people, free will, first-person language, color, ethics, organisms, and indeed life itself. Talk about cutting your face off to spite your nose! Now you may think I'm over-egging the ontological omelet a tad. But here is a taster sample. As one Nobel Prize–winning biologist put it: "Biology no longer studies life."[3] And as a philosopher of science tells us: "if we ask the question, when did human life begin? The answer is never."[4] Here are four more philosophers, first of all Paul Churchland: "Could it turn

2. Chesterton, *Orthodoxy*, 59. For a much more thorough development of all the arguments that follow, see Cunningham, *Darwin's Pious Idea*.

3. Jacob, *Logic of Life*, 299. Also see Kahane, *La vie n'existe pas!*; Shostak, *Death of Life*.

4. Ghiselin, *Metaphysics and the Origin of Species*, 1.

out that no one has ever believed anything?"[5] And Thomas Metzinger is even more to the point: "no such things as selves exist in the world: Nobody ever was or had a self."[6] And it is not just the self that is lost, for we are told that "ethics is an illusion fobbed off on us by our genes."[7] Following in the wake of the demise of ethics is that of formal thought: "Biological fitness is a function of reproductive advantages rather than a philosophical insight. Thus if we benefit biologically by being deluded about the true nature of formal thought, then so be it. A tendency to objectify is the price of reproductive success."[8] Rather tellingly, Quine once compared the simple belief in objects to belief in the gods of Homer.[9] How, if matter is all there is, can we discern *real difference between matter thus and now matter so*, even if, in our folk language, that change might be termed (parochially and indeed colloquially) as murder, cancer, and so on. This is, therefore, the very liquidation of existence.

Now, Dawkins may just tell us to pull our socks up, stiff upper lip and all that, as we just have to accept that *there is such a thing as just being plain wrong.* Maybe, for we have, it seems, been wrong indeed, presuming that people, and so on, exist. But the problem here is that there no longer seems to be anything *as being plain right!* As Patricia Churchland admits, in light of a universalized Darwinism, truth is epiphenomenal, like some shadow cast by the solid stone of evolutionary survival: "There is a fatal tendency to think of the brain as essentially in the fact-finding business. . . . Looked at from an evolutionary point of view, the principal function of nervous systems is to get the body parts where

5. Quoted in Baker, "Cognitive Suicide," 1.

6. Metzinger, *Being No One*, 1.

7. Ruse and Wilson, "Evolution of Ethics," 310.

8. Ruse, *Taking Darwin Seriously*, 188.

9. Quine, "Two Dogmas of Empiricism," 44.

they should be in order that the organism may survive . . . Truth, whatever that is, definitely takes hindmost." Many other philosophers—atheist ones, I might add—concur (for instance, Jerry Fodor, Thomas Nagel, and Barry Stroud): there is a complete disconnect between truth and survival in Darwinism, while the normative, indeed the rational, is a wine beyond the purse of naturalism's ontology, not to mention taste. In short, truth is evacuated of all content as it becomes wedded to function, and it is only the function that matters.

Take the example of congealing identity, something religion is supposed to do. But of course, National Socialism is an equal candidate for this, as is the Decalogue and indeed anything else, for success is wholly retrospective, and indifferent. The point to be understood is that in the clearest possible terms, Darwin is not in the epistemology business; in other words, it is not about knowledge, but about survival; therefore, "Evolution is neutral as to whether most of our beliefs are true. Like Rhett Butler in the movies, it just doesn't give a damn."[10]

The philosopher John Searle famously offered an argument against the idea that computers are mindful. While the content and reason of the argument bear no relevance here, the principle at work does. The argument is usually referred to as Searle's Chinese Room. Imagine someone locked in a room, someone who does not understand any Chinese. In the room there are boxes in which there are Chinese symbols. In addition, there is a rule book that instructs him how to respond to certain sets of symbols. He follows the rules and gives correct responses: "If I [the person in the Chinese room] do not understand Chinese on the basis of implementing a computer program for understanding Chinese, then neither does any other digital computer solely on that

10. Fodor, "Is Science Biologically Possible?" 42.

basis, because no digital computer has anything which I do not have."[11] The point is that the man in the room has only a grasp of syntax, and not of semantics, for the latter requires an understanding of meaning and not just the application of rules. We agree because we believe in the existence of mind, but that is irrelevant here.

Transferring Searle's argument to the question of what relation truth has with biological fitness, we can see that a syntactical grasp of Chinese is sufficient to get the job done. Moreover, a merely syntactical argument can go all the way down. In other words, there is no such thing as a semantical understanding of Chinese. We don't need it. Or, rather, natural selection does not need it. This being the case, Chinese is not about truth. There is no truth of Chinese but simply the occurrence of tasks, so to speak. Call this major task, "SEX." And we must bear in mind that any road that leads to "Rome" does, by definition, get us there, even if we thought we were going to Belfast, and even if we in fact believe that Belfast is Rome (though that's pretty hard to do). After all, Columbus never thought that he had discovered America. He had, but that was beside the point. His belief was irrelevant. It is not the case that any belief will do the job, however, but that any belief *can* do the job. And this is the case because, again, the intrinsic content of belief is irrelevant. Only its extrinsic relation to the major task—SEX—matters, as it were.[12]

Survival has the ascendancy over truth, and while truth and survival may at times coincide, such coincidence is contingent. This means that many of our most cherished beliefs have, according to those such as Dawkins, turned

11. Searle, *Mystery of Consciousness*, 11.

12. Rather disturbingly, from the ultra-Darwinian point of view, even rape can get us to "Rome," and that is just as good as any other route; see O'Hear, *Beyond Evolution*, 140.

out to be patently false. (What are memes, after all?) Moreover, many scientific views have themselves turned out to be erroneous, yet we have undoubtedly benefited from them. Falsehoods can be beneficial. Does not society (not that society exists—Margaret Thatcher obviously being a keen advocate of ultra-Darwinism) benefit from us accepting erroneous ideas like mind, existence, free will, ethics, and even objects? But we are told that none of these ideas is true. At the same time, however, we wouldn't fancy our chances crossing the road to pay a visit to our Darwinian lover without them. In short, truth is not about fitness enhancement. Any fiction that is useful is fair game for natural selection. As the Rolling Stones once sang, "you can't always get what you want, but you might just get what you need." As the saying goes, "In the kingdom of the blind, the one-eyed man is king." In our case this would be: "In the land of the dead, that which mistakenly thinks it is alive, breeds." In the movie *The Matrix*, the deluded humans are pretty damn useful for the robots (read: genes). But there, as with us, fitness does not track truth.

There we are, at Dawkins' summer camp, singing Lennon's song, but we, with our stiff upper lip, have embraced our situation and have altered the lyrics: *Imagine there's no people, it's easy if you try, no free will within us, nor life, or death, ethics, or reason, arts or sciences.* Wasn't it one of Darwin's most avid supporters, E. O. Wilson, who told us that evolution was the best myth we have? It seems true to say, then, that the truth of evolution—which I don't doubt for a moment—when uttered from within the camp of ultra-Darwinism, seems risible, for any such bid for veracity is analogous to the proverbial drunk man on a moving train who appears to walk straighter than his fellow passengers. To repeat, all truth, or that which happens to be successful, is purely accidental.

Ultra-Darwinism is, of course, underwritten by naturalism and materialism, but echoing W. B. Yeats, the center cannot hold for reductive naturalism, likewise for a universalized Darwinism. So it seems that all we are left with is what amounts to a promissory materialism, a presumptive materialism, or indeed a materialism of the gaps.[13] Like ghosts of philosophy past, we are haunted by what Bas van Fraassen calls "the spirit of materialism."[14] Or as Bertrand Russell said, "Matter has become as ghostly as anything in a spiritualist séance."[15] In short, as Noam Chomsky makes clear, we must not beg the question, for "if the scientific undertaking has limits, why should we stick on them the label 'matter,' with its old-fashioned connotations of 'extended impenetrable stuff'? Isn't it a way of hiding our ignorance?"[16] The term *matter* is, therefore, somewhat analogous to the idea of fashion: it keeps changing precisely because nothing is truly fashionable, just as there is nothing that is intrinsically true. Naturalism and materialism are, therefore, mere placeholders for the hope that there is no God. Richard Lewontin offers us two confessions regarding the relation between science and materialism: On the one hand, "it is not that the methods and institutions of science somehow compel us to accept a materialist explanation of the world, but on the contrary, that we are forced by adherence to materialist causes to create an apparatus of investigation that produces materialist explanations."[17] And

---

13. "Promissory materialism" is Popper's phrase; see Popper and Eccles, *Self and Its Brain*, 96–98. For presumptive materialism, see van Fraassen, *Empirical Stance*, 49. And lastly, for a materialism of the gaps, see Wallace, *Taboo of Subjectivity*, 128.

14. See van Fraassen, *Empirical Stance*, 58.

15. Russell, *Outline of Philosophy*, 78.

16. Bitbol, "Materialism, Stances and Open-Mindedness" 252.

17. Quoted in Le Fanu, *Why Us?*, 232.

on the other hand, "We take the side of science in spite of the patent absurdity of some of its contructs, in spite of its failures to fulfill many of its extravagant promises . . . in spite of the tolerance of the scientific community for unsubstantiated just-so stories, because we have a prior committment to materialism. . . . Moreover that materialism is absolute, for we cannot allow a Divine foot in the door."[18]

The shifting sands of materialism and its strained efforts belie hollowness, one that Nietzsche would recommend we expose with a hammer, gently tapping the sides of this modern idol, being greeted by a telling sound. This is the intractable *je ne sais quoi* of materialism and likewise of naturalism. As Barry Stroud points out, naturalism is a bit like world peace: everyone advocates it, but no one has a clue what it means.[19] But apparently, "Naturalism is supposed to be a Good Thing. So good in fact that everybody wants to be a naturalist, no matter what their views might be."[20] Or as van Fraassen tells us, "To identify what naturalism is, apart from something praiseworthy, I have found nigh-impossible. . . . Most likely it cannot be identified with any factual thesis at all."[21] Stephen Stich (who is certainly no friend of theology, not to mention the mind) compounds naturalism by issuing a challenge and a prognostication: "It is my contention that there is *no* defensible naturalistic criterion [that is, a criterion to identify a claim as naturalistic], just as there is no defensible criterion of empirical meaningfulness. . . . [If naturalists] can be provoked into proposing and criticizing criteria with the same energy that the positivists displayed, it's my bet that . . . naturalism will

18. Lewontin, "Billions and Billions of Demons," 31.

19. Stroud, "Charm of Naturalism," 22.

20. Seager, "Real Patterns and Surface Metaphysics," 95.

21. van Fraassen, "Science, Materialism, and False Consciousness," 172.

ultimately suffer the same fate as positivism did: It will die the death of a thousand failures."[22]

In light of the above, surely the most accurate definition of naturalism is probably that of hopeful naturalism (once again it is merely the frantic hope that there's no God).[23] But such wishful naturalism really won't get us very far. So there seem to be two choices. On the one hand, we can embrace naturalism, and ultra-Darwinism, the no-nonsense, hard-nosed stance that accepts the limits of naturalistic explanation no matter the consequences, even if they include incoherence, rabid skepticism, and the undermining of science. On the other hand, we can follow Stroud, who recommends a much more open form of naturalism but points out that we might just as well call it open-mindedness.

The pathology evident in naturalism and materialism is even more pronounced in one of their progeny, namely, scientism—the idea that science is the *only* arbiter of truth, even though this view is not itself a scientific one, but an extra-scientific one (in other words, it is a philosophical view). But leaving aside scientism's foundational contradiction, its danger is brought to our attention by borrowing some words of Dawkins, but changing a couple of them: "It is fashionable to wax apocalyptic about the threat to humanity posed by the AIDS virus, 'mad cow' disease, and many others, but I think the case can be made that *scientism* is one of the world's greatest evils, comparable to the smallpox virus but harder to eradicate. *Scientism*, being belief that isn't based on evidence, is the principal vice of any militant atheism."[24] We are of course substituting the word *scientism* for *faith*. Now, such scientism (which

22. Stich, *Deconstructing the Mind*, 197.

23. Seager, "Real Patterns and Surface Metaphysics," 96.

24. Quoted in McGrath, *Dawkins' God*, 84.

we can take as an umbrella term for both naturalism and ultra-Darwinism) appears to have been accommodated by an alteration in our intellectual consciousness. And this change is duly noted by Joseph Ratzinger: "The separation of physics from metaphysics achieved by Christian thinking is being steadily canceled. Everything is to become 'physics' again.'[25] This unfortunate turn, to say the least, can be seen in the words attributed to Ernest Rutherford: "There is only physics; all the rest is stamp collecting." (Poor old Darwin!) One major consequence of this is that science as a discipline becomes less rational, more reductive, and so more nihilistic, undermining itself in the process.

Let us now ask, did Darwin kill God? The answer is *Yes!* Yes, Darwin did kill God. But as has been suggested by others in relation to Nietzsche's famous claim that God was dead and that we had killed him, we can respond that the God who was discovered to be lifeless was always so. In other words, that God was always dead, and for the simple reason that it was in fact an idol. Interestingly, Darwin, unconsciously no doubt, anticipated Nietzsche, for he too killed an idol: the god of the gaps, the god of intelligent design, and the god of the creationists.

But another murder has been committed, and the perpetrators are none other than the crazy-eyed Darwinian fundamentalists, and what have they murdered? Quite simply, but shockingly, *evolution* itself. Ultra-Darwinists have killed Darwin's child, and they have done so because they are in fact lapsed religious fundamentalists, who are, by default, advocates of special creation, for like the Neanderthal they simply refuse to accept that anything can pass through the birth canal of evolution and be real. The ultra-Darwinist, therefore, resembles the fundamentalist who goes to Bible college, only to discover that Moses may

25. Ratzinger, *Truth and Tolerance*, 178.

not indeed have been the author of the Pentateuch (which should not come as that great a shock, since it contains an account of his death!) and subsequently loses faith. But he remains a fundamentalist by default, insofar as he has not thought to question the original model of truth that governs his approach to existence.

There is an old saying that offers sage advice: the theology that marries the science of today will be the widow of tomorrow. And that seems to be correct; yes, it is good and constructive for theology to engage with science, but it cannot act as its foundation, so to speak. But this also applies to atheism: *the atheism that marries the science of today will be the widow of tomorrow.* Even Dawkins admits as much, in relation to evolution: "Darwin may have been triumphant at the end of the twentieth century, but we must acknowledge the possibility that new facts may come to light which will force our successors of the twenty-first century to abandon Darwinism or modify it *beyond recognition.*"[26] But if that's the case, his use of a highly selective and inherently provisional interpretation of Darwinism as a vehicle for his own brand of atheism is wholly illegitimate, to say the least. Is this not an eminent example of what we might call "the devil of the gaps"?

Dawkins tells us that "the human psyche has two great sicknesses: the urge to carry vendetta across generations, and the tendency to fasten group labels on people rather than see them as individuals."[27] He then goes on to attribute these great sicknesses to Abrahamic religion. But this is exactly what his theory of the selfish gene perpetrates: the identity of any organism is denied validity, insofar as it is ephemeral, for only the genes are real. As a result, the organism is but a cloud or a swarm of genes—genes that

26. Dawkins, *Devil's Chaplain*, 81.
27. Ibid., 160.

have carried their own selfish vendettas across many generations. But alas, these mad fundamentalist genes do not exist. Notably, it is not the opponents of Darwinism who argue this, but rather geneticists, molecular biologists, and so on, for these researchers have dethroned the gene, that would-be atom of biology, and allocated it a rather more humble yet significant role. Today, in what is now post-genomic biology, the gene is extremely useful, but it is not in truth a fully identifiable entity, for not only are its boundaries hazy—which is to say, it is not discrete—but any noticeable effects a gene may have are also highly variable insofar as the whole process is enormously dynamic.

Just as selfish genes do not exist (or are only of a secondary order), selfishness does not exist either. It is only a "spandrel"—an architectural by-product that one might mistakenly interpret to be deliberate, or the main point of the exercise. Put another way, any selfishness there is, is derivative and not originary, while *cooperation is primary*, and don't take my word for it. All organisms, including us, are the products of such profound cooperation, for we are in fact composed of past entities that have surrendered their individuality (thus suppressing selfishness) and entered into a new dispensation, to the point that their past identity fades from all memory, and is remembered only when catastrophic betrayal occurs, so to speak.[28] A classic example is that of cancer, which abandons the individual of which it is a part and strikes out on its own, like a burglar that betrays the society into which it was born and raised, and of which it is a part. The crucial point to be made is that if selfishness were originary, evolution would never have occurred—true selfishness would consist in an

28. See Michod, "Cooperation and Conflict in the Evolution of Individuality"; Michod, *Darwinian Dynamics*; Buss, *Evolution of Individuality*.

absence of evolution—and therefore *survival would not survive*. Instead, selfishness would remain in the swamp of its birth and not bother moving, so to speak.[29] But of course, any such birth would not occur, for that would require a prior act of cooperation. To put it in Freudian terms: the only true instinct of a would-be selfish replicator would be *Thanatos* (the death instinct) because self-identity, with its precarious, finite nature, involves a central ingredient of altruism. This may seem counterintuitive, but it is patently obvious. Persistence is grounded in endless exchange, most evident in our metabolisms. We are therefore the product of *fundamental reciprocity*. In this way, the entire biological world is precisely the opposite of selfishness, which is not to say that selfishness is not present and important but that from the very fact that we can understand selfishness, we are implicitly entertaining its secondary status.

Put another way, there has to be something there to be selfish, but its existence precedes selfishness, because its coming into being is an act of gratuity, only after which is selfishness possible. Biologists refer to this as the *existence problem*, which we can think of as the *arrival of the fittest*, which then accommodates the *survival of the fittest*. We can think of it this way.[30] Evolution consists in both a theatre and a play; the play is the drama of survival (the flux of phylogeny), while the theatre, the structured environment, is the very possibility of there being a play, and that possibility, again, precedes selfishness and questions of survival, as it is the gift of that very possibility.[31] Crucially, though, the

---

29. Koslowski, "Theory of Evolution as Sociobiology and Bioeconomics," 310; Jonas, *Phenomenon of Life*, 106.

30. See Fontana and Buss, "Arrival of the Fittest"; Fontana, "Typology of the Possible," 5.

31. See Hutchinson, "Ecological Theatre and the Evolutionary Play"; Schloss, "Would Venus Evolve on Mars?" 335.

existence problem and the theatre, so to speak, do not re-side in the primordial past, but, as it were, accompany evo-lution continually, thus making possible every new exciting level of evolution and emergence. Doing so right up to the point that an animal came along that was able to write the *Origin of Species*, the Bible, and of course, *Mein Kampf.* This is the drama and risk of existence that has emerged from the womb of evolution, for there is now real blood, bodies, truth, and therefore ethics. The Zwinglian metaphysics of Neanderthals such as Dawkins must be left behind. Let us ask once again, did Darwin kill God? No. But evolution did kill ultra-Darwinism—that is, if it ever really existed.

History and Atheism

5

Empires of the Mind

ALISTER MCGRATH

Alister McGrath is a priest in the Church of England and a professor and head of the Centre for Theology, Religion and Culture at King's College, London. Before training for ministry he was a molecular biochemist, and he has written widely on historical theology and the relation of religion to science, publishing Dawkins' God: Genes, Memes, and the Meaning of Life *and* The Dawkins Delusion? *in response to the New Atheism debate. Here he focuses on the New Atheists' view of history, which presents "religion" as reactionary and dying out, while atheism is the historically inevitable and exciting future. He notes the* ad hominem *nature of much of their rhetoric, which requires a pastoral response from the Church, but also the deeper point, grasped by the prophets of ancient Israel, that against all forms of historicism, the future cannot be known and is frequently surprising. Empires of the mind, like the empires of Babylon and Assyria, will turn to dust like all the others.*

—JH

"The empires of the future will be empires of the mind." Speaking to a wartime audience at Harvard University in 1943, Winston Churchill put into words his conviction that the great dominions of the new world would not be based upon nation-states—such as the Roman or British empires—but upon ideas. Future wars would be based on ideologies, not national boundaries and agendas. Churchill may well have had in mind the astonishing power of systems—above all, Nazism and Marxism—to capture the minds and loyalties of generations.

It is difficult to read these words today without thinking of the New Atheism, whose leading representatives declare themselves to be at war with a vague generality they call "religion." This false universal called "religion" is denounced as a form of mental illness, a degenerate form of intellectual and moral pathology that must be prevented from contaminating Western culture with its toxic ideas.

Happily, a bold band of white, middle-class knights in shining armor has come to the rescue of human civilization. The "Four Horsemen"—Richard Dawkins, Daniel Dennett, Sam Harris, and Christopher Hitchens—may have recycled old ideas, but they did it with such panache and bravado that they managed to persuade the media that there was still life in the old atheist mantras of the Enlightenment.

The New Atheism has a wonderful way with sound bites. Admittedly, its noisier spokesmen—yes, they *are* all men—often seem to confuse these sharp and snappy slogans, delivered with a breathtaking confidence, with evidence-based arguments. Yet these sound bites are often deeply revealing, opening windows into the soul of the New Atheism, and allowing us to catch a glimpse of its values and ideas. "God is a delusion"—one of the more familiar and tedious of these pomposities—is not really an argument. It's an assertion that those who believe in God are mentally ill and lack even the basic intelligence to break free from a prison of their own making. Yet the real importance of the slogan lies not in its ridicule of religion, but in its affirmation of the moral and intellectual virtues of atheists. To be an atheist is to be bold, brave, brilliant, and above all *right*.

As someone who chose to become a Christian on account of my belief that atheism was intellectually and spiritually deficient in comparison, I find myself bemused by this approach. If someone were to say, "There are problems in believing in God," I would be among the first to agree—though I would want to add awkward footnotes, such as "there are problems in believing *anything*," or "there are even more problems in being an atheist." But the New Atheism seems to prefer to attack people rather than ideas. The principle is simple: "shame and embarrass people away from religion, browbeating them about the stupidity of belief in a bellicose god" (Greg Epstein). Ridicule, not argument, is the weapon of choice—unsurprisingly, since intellectual historians such as Sir Isaiah Berlin have long recognized the limitations of reason and argument in sorting out the great questions of life.

This strategy works—or at least it seems to. Many young people, acutely sensitive to the judgments of their peers, find it difficult to admit to belief in God in the face of such verbal bullying. "Are you mad enough to believe in God?" is not exactly a neutral way of beginning a conversation. That's why pastoral support for vulnerable believers matters so much. That's why churches need to realize the importance of providing and maintaining "plausibility structures" (Peter Berger) to affirm, uphold, and support people in the face of such withering scorn and intense ridicule.

Yet my concern here is to focus on one such rhetorical strategy that I have learned is integral to New Atheism apologetics. To plunder and pervert a phrase from Marxism, the New Atheism is convinced of the historic inevitability of atheism. Religion is a barbarous relic from the past; atheism is the bright, sunlit path of the future, which beckons to us to abandon irrationality and superstition and to embrace its rational and scientific certainties. People like myself, who believe in God, are portrayed as backward-looking idiots, incapable of realizing that the future is as godless as it is inevitable. Any cool, sophisticated, right-thinking person will want to adopt ideas that will dominate the future. Let's go with the flow.

It's a neat approach. Ideas about God are held to be like fashion accessories. God, we are told, is so *yesterday*. The wise want to be ahead of the curve, adopting today what everyone else will adopt tomorrow. As Karl Popper pointed out in his *Poverty of Historicism*, many are tempted to believe that coming might is right. Yet it's not. As the prophets of Israel surveyed the geopolitical landscape of their age, they realized that the political certainties of their age would be eroded. Assyria was great! Yet Assyria would fall. Babylon was great! Yet Babylon too would fall. God "brings princes to naught and reduces the rulers of this world to nothing. No sooner are they planted, no sooner are they sown, no sooner do they take root in the ground, than he blows on them and they wither, and a whirlwind sweeps them away like chaff" (Isa 40:23–24).

In the twentieth century, Marxism gained sway over half the world following the Second World War, only to falter and fade. Yet for many in the 1930s, this was the future—intellectually fashionable and politically radical. The historically inevitable, however, turned out to be the historically contingent. Few have failed to note the new cultural and political significance of Christianity in post-Soviet Russia, or its recent rapid rise to intellectual and social influence in the People's Republic of China.

The New Atheism presents its own triumph as a historical inevitability. It's an assertion that beguiles the foolish and entrances the followers of fashion. Yet for the rest of us, it is highly questionable. The idea of "historical inevitability" is a sociological judgment, which has little to do with what is intellectually or morally right or wrong. As the prophets of Israel knew full well, what may seem to be a permanent shift often turns out to be a passing historical phase. Even the natural sciences are prone to the radical changes of judgment that Thomas Kuhn rightly pronounced to be "paradigm shifts." Today, most scientists believe that the universe had an origin. A hundred years ago, most believed it had been around forever. What will they believe in the future? And for how long?

So what *does* the future hold? "Nobody knows the future—least of all those who believe in historical determinism" (Joseph Brodsky). Christianity has to take the long view—thinking in terms of centuries, not years. None of us sees the "big picture," which allows us to grasp the significance of our present moment in the greater scheme of things. We have to trust that, despite the cultural and social pressures for secularism and unbelief in Western Europe, greater and deeper forces are at work. We cannot prove that this is the case, even to ourselves. But what we *can* do is take that deeper and broader view that we find in Israel's prophets.

As the prophets saw the empires of the world rise and fall, they reflected long and hard on what really mattered, and above all, what really was timeless. Human ideas and human power would ultimately fade away. The big question was whether there was anything that remained constant and reliable across the vast expanses of human history. We know their answer. "The grass withers and the flowers fade, but the word of our God stands forever" (Isa 40:8). If Christianity is right, it *must* survive—and *must* continue to speak to the hearts, minds, and imaginations of humanity. As Augustine put it in his celebrated prayer: "you have made us for yourself, and our heart is restless until it finds its rest in you."

Perhaps we do live in dark and uncertain times, when the future seems uncertain and the flame of faith seems to flicker. But that is not the full story. The Christian faith tells us that our individual stories are part of a greater narrative, which we grasp only partially and dimly. What we do *matters*, even though we cannot know its final outcomes or significance.

In the end, all empires—whether political or intellectual—fall and fade, leaving those who believed in them and relied upon them wondering where to turn next. Our task is to sow the seeds of hope and to challenge, graciously yet firmly, the claims to finality of the ideologies of the present. We must keep the cause of faith alive today, believing that others who follow us in the future will make it flourish. And we must trust that God will take our widow's mite and transmute it into gold, as we try to witness to faith in our cynical and dismissive age.

6

Christianity's Bastard Child

JOHN HUGHES

John Hughes is Dean of Chapel and Fellow at Jesus College. He is a priest in the Church of England and teaches philosophy and ethics in the Cambridge University Faculty of Divinity. He has published on the relationship between Christianity and Marxism (The End of Work: Theological Critiques of Capitalism).
In this sermon I argue that, although the vehemence of the New Atheism is a response to the contemporary geopolitical situation, in other ways its tone is typically Anglo-Saxon, Protestant, and liberal. Such a perspective helps us see atheism as another historically contingent worldview rather than the "natural" default position. It can also help us engage in more sophisticated conversation, recognizing that certain atheist distortions of Christianity began with Christians themselves. Finally, I suggest that unlike other religions, in the cross Christianity has a particular way of speaking about

the atheist experience of a world apparently without God and the atheist rebellion against God.

—JH

Amos 9:5–end; Ephesians 6:1–20

"Be strong in the Lord . . . for we are not contending against flesh and blood . . ."

What does Christianity have to do with atheism?[1] We can begin by asking what is peculiar, what is "new" about the New Atheists. What is the *history* of atheism? Atheism itself, of course, is nothing new, being found in various forms in the ancient world, and enjoying considerable fashion in certain Western intellectual circles for at least the last century or two. One thing that is remarkable about the new strain, however, is its virulence, the sheer strength of its loathing of religion and its desire to eradicate it from the face of the earth. As Eagleton suggested in his sermon in this volume, this is probably a reaction to the surprising *resurgence* of religion in geopolitics and even in the West in the last twenty years. Lofty scorn toward religion, such as was found in many mid-twentieth-century Oxbridge dons, is fine for something that you believe to be dying out; but if you think the disease is spreading, then fiercer action may be needed. This already suggests that the history of atheism

1. This way of thinking about atheism is influenced by the work of Henri de Lubac (*Drama of Atheist Humanism*) and Alasdair MacIntyre (see especially *After Virtue* and *Whose Justice? Which Rationality?*).

may be more symbiotically bound up with that of religion than either might like to admit (more of this in a moment).

The other thing that particularly characterizes the *New* Atheists is what we might call their Anglo-Saxon temperament. By this I mean a particular combination of, on the one hand, not even taking religion very seriously, seeing it as something silly that makes very little difference to life either way; combined on the other hand, with a rather complacent lack of awareness regarding the provenance of their own worldview, which is seen as somehow self-evident to all sensible chaps. As a number of our preachers have noticed, you only have to contrast this with the great continental atheists such as Sade, Nietzsche, Marx, or Sartre to see just how very "English" this style of atheism is. These continental thinkers were much more aware of how Christianity had shaped the values and thought of the West in ways almost too subtle to notice, and how if one were to abandon God, then everything would look different. You will probably have gathered by now that I think these continental atheists make much more interesting dialogue partners for religion, because they at least understand what is at stake, unlike the polite drawing-room English atheists, for whom the news that there is no God seems about as significant as if someone had told them the cricket had been rained off. This "Anglo-Saxon" atheism goes back quite some way—we can see traces of it in Hume or George Eliot—but it is nevertheless a product of a *particular culture and history*, not the universal self-evident position that it sometimes makes itself out to be. Indeed, when Bertrand Russell quipped that he was a "*Protestant* atheist" rather than a Catholic one, he was touching on something very important. Anglo-Saxon atheism has a very Protestant, at times even Puritan, ethos. It is classically liberal, affirming human freedom and progress, and suspicious of all tradition and authority. And it would not be unfair, I think, to suggest that it often has a rather limited bourgeois aesthetic sensibility; it is suspicious of images and metaphors, in a way that can incline towards philistinism in its love of brute facts. A passage such as we heard in our first reading about "the mountains dripping sweet wine" just sounds silly to such a mentality. This Anglo-Saxon atheism is also, to be fair, often very high-minded in its moralism, almost trying to be *more* Christian than Christianity, so that ironically it will attack Christians for failing to live up to their own ideals. Recognizing this *Christian* provenance of much modern atheism can help contemporary debates in a number of ways. First, to recognize that atheism has a *history* is to see that atheism is not simply the natural, neutral default position that everyone would have held if they had not been indoctrinated by some religion or other. This, in turn, can help put the debate back on a more equal footing: it becomes a debate between two views rather than between common sense and madness. Indeed, I would go further and suggest that the very word *religion*, which in its contemporary sense is a relatively modern construct, is largely unhelpful and would be best dispensed with.[2] If we speak instead of worldviews, or something similar, we might begin to recognize that *everyone*, whether they are "religious" or not, has views on the nature of ultimate reality, which are, in the final instance, a matter of *faith*, or interpretation, beyond mere proof. We can describe something in terms of its genetic codes or in terms of mass or energy, and these descriptions are extremely clever, precise, and useful; but they are not the *only*, or the *ultimate*, way of describing reality.

Secondly, however, recognizing that atheism has a particular history that relates it to Christianity can help genuine dialogue by enabling atheists to see that some of

2. See Lash, *Beginning and End of "Religion."*

their most cherished values are the fruit of the Christian tradition. (This can be particularly difficult to see because of how pervasive Christian values still are in the modern world, making them seem simply universal and self-evident rather than distinctively Christian.) For their part, Christians might see that some of the atheists' objections to religion have their roots in Christianity itself. Some of our other preachers have alluded to this, and it would take too long to spell it all out here tonight, but in brief, Christians would do well to remember that if atheists sometimes talk as if God were some distant clockmaker, or a brutal tyrant, then this is probably because certain Christians did so first! Likewise, if the New Atheists treat the Scriptures in a completely ahistorical way, like some encyclopedia dropped from the skies, then it is probably because there were already Christians doing exactly the same thing. If this is so, then atheism can serve to recall Christians to our traditions, to look at where things may have gone awry, and to recover more authentic accounts of what we believe.

Some writers have gone even further than this on the relationship between Christianity and atheism. Given the way that, in the scope of world history, atheism, far from being the universal default, is actually the more unusual option, they have suggested that Judaism and Christianity actually helped pave the way for atheism, with ideas such as the rejection of all idols, the incarnation (God becomes human), and the crucifixion (God dies). On some accounts, then, Christianity is destined to become atheistic.[3] It won't surprise you, I hope, to discover that I do not take this view. But, I think, there is a half-truth here: Christianity does have a special attitude in relation to atheism that sets it apart from other religions. Christians believe that God does

3. This Hegelian thought is developed by various "Death of God" theologians such as Gianni Vattimo.

not force himself upon us, that he does leave us the freedom to respond to him in faith or not. This is one of the reasons why Christians must take atheists seriously: because God has given us this freedom to say no to him.

But it does not stop there: at the heart of Christianity stands the cross, where God the incarnate Son cries out, "My God, my God, why hast thou forsaken me?" In this extraordinary, incomprehensible event, at which the drawing-room atheist might well shake his head in disbelief, God is alienated from Godself and experiences the depths of despair. Here God takes upon Godself our rejection of him and bears it for us. Atheism is then not just something to which Christianity can simply be opposed. According to the Christian faith, God takes into himself *even* the rebellion against himself that is atheism. Within the life of any believer, there are moments of doubt and despair, moments in which we experience isolation from God, as Christ did upon the cross. But in Christ, we believe that *even* this cannot separate us from God.

Because of this, we can say, by way of conclusion, that Christians should not be overly anxious or defensive towards even the most vehement and aggressive atheism, because if we are right, then it is almost impossible to live a life completely in opposition to God, whatever people may say with their lips. When we hear the language of battle used in relation to Christianity, as in our second reading from Ephesians, or in the hymn "Onward Christian Soldiers," we should not be misled into taking this literally as calling for some crusade against unbelievers. As Paul says, "we are not contending against flesh and blood"; hence the weapons that are needed are simply "the belt of truth," "the breastplate of justice," "the helmet of salvation," and "the sword of the Spirit." There is a place for arguments and debates, but finally it will be through the testimony of lives lived that hearts may be changed—lives that enter into the experience of those who reject them and, instead of returning opposition, return love, as God himself does upon the cross.

Suffering and Hope

7

Morality, Tragedy, and Imagination

JOHN CORNWELL

John Cornwell was raised a Roman Catholic and attended seminary with the intention of becoming a priest. He left the seminary and later became an agnostic until recovering his faith twenty years later. He has had a career as an author and journalist, and runs the Rustat conferences at Jesus College, including the Science and Human Dimension project. He published Darwin's Angel: An Angelic Riposte to the God Delusion, *his playful response to Dawkins, in 2007, developing themes from two previous articles. In this sermon he reflects on the adversarial style of the contemporary media and its impact upon the New Atheist debate, before offering his own alternative way of staging this conversation through the discussion of evil and suffering in Dostoevsky's famous* Brothers Karamazov. *Christians should share with Ivan the horror at the world's cruelties and injustices, but ultimately the most eloquent response is not to be found in rationalistic arguments but in the counter-witness of a life such as Alyo-sha's. He concludes by finding these themes echoed in the writings of John Henry Newman, where he also sees a recognition of the importance of imagination beyond pure reason alone.*

—JH

I have been wondering whether, by reflecting on the New Atheist debate as a media phenomenon, one can reach a better understanding of what has been going on. A former and sadly lamented late colleague, Nicholas Tomalin, one-time Middle East correspondent, was famous for his harsh verdict on the denizens of the media: "The only qualities essential for real success in journalism," he once wrote, "are ratlike cunning, a plausible manner, and a little literary ability."[1] Tomalin was a brave and accomplished writer, and modest with it. He was killed by a rocket while reporting the Yom Kippur War in Israel in 1973. His name appears alongside the names of two thousand others of his profession at the Bayeux memorial to journalists killed while on journalistic action since the Second World War, and their number continues to grow. Yet there is, of course, more than a grain of truth in Tomalin's acerbic description of journalism, especially of the "opinion" practitioners who run no risks to life, limb, or reputation, and are rather well paid for routinely parading their personal prejudices rather than delivering objective reports.

Tomalin's characterization of journalism is worth bearing in mind when reflecting on the so-called New

1. Tomalin, *Nicholas Tomalin Reporting*, 77.

Atheist debate. For those on both sides of this debate have been drawn into antagonistic postures set by the constraints and the pretensions of the media. Issues within the media ambit, especially the rules of polemic on programs like *Today*, *Newsnight*, and *Question Time*, favor the plausible, the cunning, and the articulate. The point of the exercise is to establish hostile, mutually exclusive polar opposites in order to create a good row, which, with a bit of luck, will end in a trouncing humiliation for a personality on one side or other.

I want to take for my theme the phenomenon of argumentative confrontation in set-piece media debates about God. And I shall focus on a recurring issue known technically as "theodicy." If God is all-loving, how can he allow a world with so much suffering? Surely, if he were all-powerful, he could end the suffering? So if he is all-loving, surely he cannot be all-powerful. And if he is all-powerful, then he cannot be all-loving. In Dostoyevsky's novel *The Brothers Karamazov*, this question is raised in the confrontation between two brothers.[2] Ivan, the elder of the brothers, seems to say at one point in their argument that if God does not exist, then everything is permitted. In other words, a world without belief in God is bound to be a world of unbridled crime and sin. Both Richard Dawkins and Christopher Hitchens invoke this reflection, as do many other public exponents of atheism, as an extremely crass viewpoint routinely cited by religious believers. Dawkins actually attributes such a viewpoint to Dostoyevsky himself: "It seems to me to require quite a low self-regard," Dawkins writes, "to think that, should belief in God suddenly vanish from the world, we would all become callous and selfish hedonists,

---

2. I am grateful to Ralph C. Wood and his article "Ivan Karamazov's Mistake" in *First Things* (December 2002) for his insights into Dostoyevsky and atheism.

with no kindness, no charity, no generosity, nothing that would deserve the name of goodness. It is widely believed that Dostoevsky was of that opinion."[3]

Dawkins adds that he himself has therefore inclined towards a less cynical view of human nature than the great Fyodor Dostoyevsky: "Do we really need policing—whether by God or by each other—in order to stop us from behaving in a selfish and criminal manner? I want to believe that I do not need such surveillance—and nor, dear reader, do you."[4] But there is a gulf between Dostoyevsky's invocation of the "no God, no morality" statement and Dawkins' understanding of what Dostoyevsky is doing in the novel.

Dostoyevsky began writing *Brothers Karamazov* in 1878, aged fifty-seven. As a child he had suffered the loss of both parents (it is believed that his father was murdered), and in his thirties he spent five years in prison, including several months on death row and four years as a convict in a labor camp. He was an epileptic, a state of health not helped by being subjected to a mock execution, facing a firing squad from which he was reprieved at the last moment. He was alleged to have been a member of a liberal underground society.

Dostoyevsky had firsthand knowledge of much tragedy and suffering: a Russian mid-nineteenth-century labor camp, overcrowded, lacking food and hygiene, and infested with lice and disease. In his forties he tried to make sense of all that darkness and violence in the light of influential ideas from the West. These included the English utilitarianism of Bentham and Stuart Mill, utopian Marxism, and the early manifestations of Social Darwinism. Dostoyevsky struggled, moreover, to understand how Christianity could withstand the new Russian nihilism (which rejected all

3. Dawkins, *God Delusion*, 259.
4. Ibid., 260.

forms of religion, morality, and politics). The conflicts and tensions between these competing ideologies and religion are dramatized at length in his great novels, not least in the fictional character Ivan Karamazov.

Ivan has traveled and immersed himself in Western thought and literature. He is a convinced atheist, who voices many of the intellectual scruples that assailed Dostoyevsky, but hardly parallel the author's entire thinking as Ivan's creator. While Ivan is acquainted with arguments for and against the existence of God, his atheism has less to do with science, reasoned proofs, and philosophy than his consciousness of the "human tears with which the earth is saturated from its crust to its center." He remains avidly curious about current affairs, but he is convinced that human existence is pointless. He has become self-absorbed, self-reliant, and supercilious, judgmental of his fellows and every attempt to justify the existence of God.

In opposition to Ivan's worldview there is the saintly monk, Father Zosima, who teaches through the example of Jesus that one must love nonjudgmentally, unconditionally, and universally as well as particularly. The meaning of life for Father Zosima is to be found in the rejection of egoism.

In the set-piece argument about the existence or nonexistence of God, Ivan's younger brother Alyosha speaks for Father Zosima's teaching while Ivan explains the reasons for his atheism. Alyosha has not traveled, nor has he read widely and deeply in Western politics, philosophy, and science. He has entered the monastery to be taught a different kind of wisdom by Father Zosima, although he fully intends to enter the world in time.

In their extraordinary confrontation, which turns out not to be a debate at all (as we shall see), Ivan does not indict God for natural disasters in the world, disease, earthquakes and so forth, since he can accept, in theory, that these trials, should God exist, might have a divine purpose—to purge and to test the human race. What Ivan cannot stomach is a God who has given adult humans the freedom to inflict suffering on children. Ivan is not so much saying: take away God and everything is permitted; he is saying that he *knows* that God does not exist, and that is *why* adults have the freedom to abuse children.

To demonstrate this circumstance, Ivan tells Alyosha that he has made a journalistic collection of atrocities, "certain interesting little facts . . . from newspapers and books . . . certain jolly little anecdotes," as Ivan puts it with heavy irony. They are cuttings taken from actual newspaper reports: soldiers who sliced babies from their mother's wombs and impaled them on their bayonets; a father and a mother who stuffed feces in the mouth of their five-year-old daughter and locked her in an outdoor lavatory all night for having wet the bed; a Russian general who ordered his hounds to tear to pieces an eight-year-old boy because he had accidentally wounded the paw of one of his dogs.

For Ivan there is no possible religious argument, including hell for the perpetrators, that would justify the existence of a God who permits such savagery against children. "It is not worth one little tear of that tortured little girl who beat herself on the breast and prayed to her 'dear, kind Lord' in the stinking privy with her unexpiated tears." Any attempt, Ivan goes on, to justify God's creation of this freedom to abuse is an insult to these innocent victims.

Alyosha listens to his brother with sympathy and understanding, but he says precisely nothing. He remains silent, yet it is not a hostile or supercilious silence. The circumstance points back to the story of the Grand Inquisitor, earlier in the novel, in which the cardinal cross-examines a silent Jesus Christ, who has revisited earth to be imprisoned as a heretic, indicating that clerical Christian religionists are equally capable of a hectoring style of "interview," even of the Son of God himself.

Alyosha's "reply" to his brother comes not in the form of a counterargument of the kind offered in the New Atheist public debates, nor the halting ripostes to the inquisitions of those such as John Humphrys or Jeremy Paxman. Alyosha's "argument" is enacted and exemplified in his entire life's project, as is Ivan's, through to the end of the narrative. The novel is not, in the hands of Dostoyevsky, a source of useful debating points. As Iris Murdoch puts it, "The novel itself, of course, the whole world of the novel, is the expression of a world outlook . . . a moral world . . ."[5]

The brothers could not be more different: Dostoyevsky's theodicy "argument" is to be located in this difference. Unlike Ivan, who boasts that he possesses a Euclidian mind—a Westernized scientific and mathematical mind—Alyosha has become practiced in a Russian Orthodox spirituality, open to the imaginative influence of God in the world. For him the Euclidean parallel lines of the spiritual and material, deemed separate into infinity, coalesce and intertwine. This kind of spirituality is not amenable, obviously, to empirical proof, nor even to rational argument, but to a lived sense of God's presence in the world exemplified in the mysticism of the Orthodox icon. The icon, crafted to the sound of hymns and of prayer, is not so much a representation of the spiritual realm as a manifestation of divine presence radiating out, and penetrating, the world: it looks *out,* rather than being looked *at.*

After Father Zosima dies, Alyosha becomes transfigured by a sense of God's radiating presence, which comes in the form of a gift rather than by his own spiritual striving or attainment. All that is necessary is openness to the gift. "The silence of the earth seemed to merge with the silence

5. Dooley, *From a Tiny Corner in the House of Fiction,* 92.

of the heavens, the mystery of the earth to be touched by the mystery of the stars. . . . It was as if threads from all those innumerable worlds of God all came together in his soul." In consequence Alyosha experiences an overpowering inclination to nonjudgmental, communal love.

As the novel progresses, Alyosha does not collect stories of children's sufferings, even though he is horrified by Ivan's reports of abuse. He seeks to find actual suffering children and to identify with them in practice, coping with the problem of evil and suffering in action, rather than the knockdown arguments of apologetics that attempt to justify the ways of God to man.

By the end of the novel Alyosha is revealed as an icon of Christ. Yet Alyosha vociferously resists any praise for his deeds. Only Christ, he responds, is deserving of worship since he is the only human being who has suffered and lost everything for the sake of others. Hence only Christ can forgive everything—even those who have tortured and murdered children.

The elementary mistake made by both Dawkins and Hitchens, who have seized on the supposed Dostoyevskian argument of "no God, no morality" and reduced it to absurdity as a point in the anti-religion debate, is to confuse the statement of a character within a novel with the complex artistic overview of its author. And there is a deeper failure, in my opinion, reflected in Terry Eagleton's contribution to this series. It is the failure to recognize the creative process within art, the novelist as creator, as an echo or shadow of a sense of creation on the edge of human consciousness: what Samuel Taylor Coleridge called "counterfeit infinity."

George Steiner, in his powerful book *Real Presences*, speculated twenty years ago that with the declining sense of the presence of the Creator on the horizon of human consciousness, it may be difficult for art to survive. More recently he has written that the challenge for the New Atheists is to produce a work of art that contains no lingering evidence of that consciousness of creation or createdness. Is that not the way, he asks, for the New Atheists to exemplify their convictions?

But the quarrel between the two brothers in the novel suggests something further to me. We have witnessed a rather different clash between two brothers on the existence or nonexistence of God in the public debates between the two Hitchens brothers, Christopher and Peter. It became a spectacle on chat shows at the height of the New Atheist spat, both brothers attempting to clobber each other with heated knockdown arguments, mainly over theodicy. And the Hitchens dispute reminds me in turn of another brotherly debate—that between John Henry Newman and his younger brother Charles in the mid-nineteenth century. In that case, however, the antagonism was resolved in time and with maturity. When Newman was a young ordained priest, he heard that his young brother had been attacking religion. A correspondence ensued in which Newman offered a string of apologetic arguments well laced with finger-wagging sermons.[6] His brother, a socialist and an agnostic, was unmoved. In the end Newman roundly accused his brother of insanity. It took the boys' mother to counsel brotherly love and patience, especially on John Henry's part.

With the passage of time Newman was to alter his opinion about how to engage the atheism of his day, with a brother or anybody else. In a sermon delivered to Oxford undergraduates in the 1830s, he suggested that one should welcome, and listen carefully to, the views of atheists, as doing so could only broaden and deepen the faith of the believer. "When a person for the first time hears the

6. Newman, *Letters and Diaries of John Henry Newman*, 1:212–15.

arguments and speculations of unbelievers, and feels what a very novel light they cast upon what he has hitherto accounted most sacred, it cannot be denied that, unless he is shocked and closes his ears and heart to them, he will have a sense of expansion and elevation."

This was no ultraliberal relativistic reflection, indicating that "there is a lot, after all, to be said for atheism." Newman was convinced ahead of Dostoyevsky's creation that a creative silence may well be the only response. On another occasion, he wrote: "The most powerful arguments for Christianity do not convince, only silence . . . I do not assert that the Christian evidences are overpowering, but that they are unanswerable."

The silence he had in mind was not a blank silence, or a sulk, or a supercilious, "this is all beneath my contempt" silence. It was a silence that created space for the heart through the imagination. While engaged in a polemic over religion and adult education in the 1830s, Newman uttered a plea, in a letter to the *Times*, for the engagement of a person's total humanity in religious conviction, practice, and argument. "The heart is commonly reached," he wrote, "not through the reason, but through the imagination, by means of direct impressions, by the testimony of facts and events, by history, by description. Persons influence us, voices melt us, looks subdue us, deeds inflame us."

It is another way of saying that our religious convictions are shown rather than stated. And this brings us full circle: for it was facts, events, history—rather than cosmological proofs—that led Ivan to his convictions against God, and it was the person of Father Zosima that melted, subdued, and inflamed Alyosha's heart.

For me, Dostoyevsky seems to be saying that there is something of an Ivan and something of an Alyosha, potentially, in suspension and in internal dialogue, in all of us.

There are no guarantees that our experience of the world, including the influences of religion, will lead us toward God; but the novelist can show how two opposing mental forces can exist within a single worldview, as if they were two aspects of a single mind, like two close but very different brothers within a single family in conversation with each other.

Maturity, or ripeness, for a person of faith, is not of course to dither endlessly between the opposing views. It is to take the option of faith, while remaining silently sympathetic to the predicament of Ivan.

8

Difficult Teachings?

TINA BEATTIE

Tina Beattie is professor of Catholic Studies at the University of Roehampton. She is a Roman Catholic who has worked on questions of theology and gender as well as on natural law and human rights. Her book The New Atheists: The Twilight of Reason and the War on Religion *(2007) remains one of the best overviews of the New Atheism. In this sermon Tina recognizes the potential criticisms of religion that could arise out of the scriptural texts appointed for the day—an apparently tyrannical God, religion as false consolation or repressive Puritanism—but then she offers alternative readings. She stresses the distinctive emphasis of the Old Testament prophets on divine justice and links this to contemporary political and economic crises, arguing that private virtue is not separable from these concerns of public justice. In response to Marxist criticisms of religion, she recognizes that although religion has behaved like an opiate when it idealizes unnecessary suffering, yet it still possesses the resources for a hope in the midst of the world's suffering that is more radical than the glib optimism of the New Atheists.*

—JH

Amos 3:1–8; Ephesians 5:1–17; Psalm 13

When I looked at the readings for this evening, I decided that not only must there be a God, but he is definitely on Richard Dawkins' side. If I had handpicked three readings to illustrate the main arguments that the New Atheists offer against religion, I might have chosen these three. First, the prophet Amos portrays God as a tyrant who must be obeyed and who punishes his chosen ones for their disobedience. Read on in Amos beyond the verses we heard tonight, and God's threats against Israel get worse and worse. Richard Dawkins and others repeatedly insist that the God of the Old Testament is, to quote Dawkins, "arguably the most unpleasant character in all fiction: jealous and proud of it; a petty, unjust, unforgiving control-freak."[1] At first glance Amos's God isn't far removed from that portrayal.

Next, the psalmist laments the fact that God seems oblivious to his suffering and fails to answer his prayers, and then affirms that nevertheless, he will keep trusting in God and singing God's praise. Another criticism leveled by the New Atheists is that religious believers insist on believing that there is a God despite all the evidence to the contrary, which is irrational. The psalmist seems to be clinging

1. Dawkins, *God Delusion*, 31.

to an obstinate and irrational faith that belies the evidence of his own experience.

Lastly, the reading from Ephesians trots out all the old injunctions against fornication and having a good time, confirming the New Atheists in their claims that Christianity is anti-sex and thoroughly repressive.

I had been told that I could choose different readings if I wanted to, and when I read through these that was very tempting. But one of the problems with a certain kind of liberal Christianity is that it becomes a pick 'n' mix affair, a bit like browsing the sweets counter at Woolworths (a name that will soon mark out people of a certain generation and show our age). One can gather a bag of goodies from the Bible that are sweet and good to chew on, but it's not much of a balanced spiritual diet. Life confronts us with much that is far from sweet and good, and the Scriptures were written by people like us who, however inspired, were grappling to understand how their visions of justice and peace and their yearning for joy could be squared with the often harsh realities of life as we know it.

So with this in mind, I want to go back to those readings for tonight, and to let them speak to us in the idiom of our own time, and with a view to the questions that we pose to our faith today. I'm going to focus on three themes: justice, with reference to Amos; hope, with reference to the psalmist; and virtue, with reference to Ephesians.

Whenever we read of God's anger and punishment in the Old Testament, we must remember that this is a God whose abiding characteristics are justice, love, and compassion. To disobey God is to violate God's justice. It's to allow greed, wealth, and power to distort our relationships with one another, so that the lives of the poor are sacrificed to the demands of the rich and the powerful. The contrite, the humble, and the merciful always find a way back to God and are welcomed, in the Old as well as the New Testament; and God repeatedly assures the poor and the oppressed that he has heard their cry, that ultimately they are neither forsaken nor abandoned. Dawkins falls into the trap of many generations of Christian interpreters, by suggesting that the Old Testament offers a particularly nasty and violent portrayal of God. Lurking within such readings, whether or not it is intended, there is a disturbing anti-Judaic prejudice that is acknowledged by many modern biblical scholars.

But the consolation God offers is, as the psalmist observes, often hidden and even absent when justice is lacking. Amos, like the other Old Testament prophets, suggests that when a society turns away from the justice that God offers, the whole of that society suffers, the innocent as well as the guilty. Is this really so hard for us to understand today? We don't speak much of God in the public forum of British life, but we speak a great deal about The Market and The Economy. These are our latter-day tyrants that must be obeyed and that will punish us all if we don't do what they demand. But unlike the God of the Old Testament, these are not transcendent sources of justice that command our allegiance. They are abstract ideologies used to justify injustice and exploitation. The author of Ephesians warns the early Christians against idolatry—which he equates with greed—and Jesus warns us that we cannot serve both God and Mammon. It isn't very hard to find parallels between these readings and our own society.

As we ourselves know, when fundamental principles of justice are abandoned, everybody suffers. When the idolatry of greed is allowed to govern our lives, we experience a sense of social disintegration and of abstract forces spiraling out of control. Here, of course, is where the psalmist's lament becomes a poignant meditation on a truth of our world. In the face of injustice, it would be deeply satisfying if the oppressors were punished and their victims were consoled and liberated. But that's not how the world seems to work. In our neo-Darwinian economics, the superrich are insulated while those at the bottom of the pile suffer most acutely and most unjustly. It's in such situations that so many of the psalms cry out to a God who seems to be absent, who seems to abandon the victims and protect their oppressors. In the face of such evidence, the psalmist repeatedly reminds himself and us that God is good, that justice will prevail.

Karl Marx's criticism of religion was directed against that promise of justice in a world to come. Religion is the opium of the people because, in offering consolation, it makes the poor compliant in the face of their exploitation, and protects the rich from the judgment of history. Marx's books have been enjoying new popularity since the beginning of the economic crisis. Christians should be the first to recognize that an idea that seems to have suffered catastrophic failure can rise back to life and gain new energy and vision.

If Christianity is not to be vulnerable to Marx's criticism and to the criticisms of the New Atheists, which come from a different angle but which also see religion as a force against rather than for justice in our world, then we must differentiate between avoidable and unavoidable suffering. Too often Christianity in the past has failed to make that distinction. There's a theology of sacrifice that has produced a masochistic cult of suffering in many expressions of Christianity. There are many people in our world, and in our own society, who are in the pits of despair because they are victims of injustice, neglect, exploitation, and oppression and see no way out of their situation. But these are humanly inflicted sufferings, and their remedy lies in our human will to act against the forces of injustice. For the churches to say to such people that they should follow the example of the psalmist, praise God, and look forward to a future justice, is I believe to invite the kind of criticism that Marx offers, substituting an otherworldly piety for an incarnate reality that demands that we take very seriously the material conditions of life.

But this also entails looking to ourselves and asking what role we play as individuals in colluding with the forces of injustice because it suits us to do so. If we take the economic crisis, for example, we know that the power of bankers and corporate shareholders far exceeds the power of political democracy in our modern world. We applaud the democratic revolutions in the Middle East, while failing to recognize how profoundly our own democratic system has been destroyed. But many of us have been complicit in that destruction. The unrestrained borrowing and consumerism of the last two decades may have been driven by the banks and by economic policies, but they pandered to common human failings of greed and acquisitiveness, and many of us played a part, however small, in creating the circumstances that led to the crisis.

When a society plunges into crisis, rarely is it solely the fault of a few corrupted leaders and their wealthy and powerful benefactors and patrons. It's usually the consequence of complex and widespread failures in individual values and behavior. This brings me to the reading from Ephesians.

One of the problems with liberalism is that it severs the link between the private and the public, the personal and the political, so that we fail to recognize the ways in which our individual pursuit of virtue is part of the fabric of the virtuous society. A society in which individuals lack virtue is a society that lacks justice. We might think here of the expenses scandal of 2009–2010. Many of our British

Members of Parliament behaved in ways that were not determined by their sense of personal integrity and accountability to the people who elected them, but by a legalistic attitude apparently evacuated of any sense of moral responsibility, which was not about what one should do but about how much one could get away with.

Ephesians reminds us that how we behave in the most intimate details of our lives—in our closest friendships, in our communities, and in our relationships, including our sexual relationships—is as important as larger political questions of justice and responsibility. A society in which each and every person seeks to affirm the dignity of every other person, in which all our relationships are marked by a sense of integrity and care for the other, will be a just society. A society that closes off huge segments of human life behind the barriers of privacy and says that anything goes in that domain, ultimately is likely to collapse in on itself, for it lacks the solid substance of personal virtue on which justice and solidarity depend. And that is when people might well find themselves with nothing and nobody but God to turn to, when the lament of the psalmist becomes the lament of the human abandoned by society.

But no matter how just a society we create, and no matter how successful we are in eliminating the most immediate causes of poverty, illness, and deprivation, suffering is part of life. In Dawkins' buoyant conclusion to *The God Delusion*, he declares himself "thrilled to be alive at a time when humanity is pushing against the limits of understanding. Even better, we may eventually discover that there are no limits."[2] Would we still be human in a world in which our understanding had become limitless? Would we then be able to give a satisfactory explanation for our most profound questions about the meaning of life? To be human is

2. Dawkins, *God Delusion*, 374.

to discover ourselves in the midst of an unanswerable mystery about who we are and why we are the kind of creatures we are. How can we explain consciousness, which enables us to break free of the necessities and laws of the natural world of which we are a part in order to imagine different worlds and possibilities? I suspect that my cat is closer to Dawkins' limitless understanding than I am or ever want to be, because only a creature enmeshed within the finite horizons of animality, deprived of freedom and imagination, could be endowed with all the knowledge it ever wanted or needed.

The hubristic confidence of the New Atheism marks it out from the darker and more brooding forms of atheism that one finds in continental philosophy and literature, from *The Brothers Karamazov* to the writings of post-Holocaust thinkers and the novels of writers such as Albert Camus. In Dawkins' world, we don't need God because the steady march of scientific progress will bring us all the answers we ever seek. It's a different form of atheism that hands back the ticket, as Dostoyevsky's Ivan does, refusing to accept the goodness of God in a world of such suffering.

Science cannot solve the mystery of suffering. It could only do so if it removed from human consciousness all our capacity for imagination, creativity, and wonder. Paradoxically, it's often in the deepest mystery of suffering that humanity encounters the deepest mystery of God. Perhaps recognizing that is the genius of Christianity's crucified God. What would art, music, and literature be without pathos, loss, and yearning? Imagine being trapped forever within the pages of *Hello* magazine, listening to Abba on your earphones.

Literary critic and Jewish agnostic George Steiner says of hope that "there is no word less deconstructible."[3] The

3. Steiner, *Real Presences*, 232.

psalmist offers us hope, not as an escape from the suffering and reality of life, but as a quality that imbues the here and now with a sense of meaning, a sense of futurity without which it's hard to imagine what it would mean to be human. This is not an otherworldly optimism that turns its back on the world, but a faith in the God of justice, love, and peace who transcends all the material conditions of history and infuses them with an abiding hope.

We bear responsibility, individually and collectively, for patterning our lives around what we know to be factual (science), what we understand to be truthful (philosophy and theology), and what we hope to be eternal (faith).

The True Revolution

9

The Timidity of the New Atheists

DAVID BENTLEY HART

David Bentley Hart is one of America's most lively contemporary Christian apologists and an Eastern Orthodox theologian who has written on the challenge of evil and suffering (The Doors of the Sea, 2005) *and on the New Atheists* (Atheist Delusions: The Christian Revolution and Its Fashionable Enemies, 2009). *In this sermon he reiterates the argument of his book that the New Atheism, far from being daring and provocative, is in fact characterized by "bourgeois respectability" and is entirely in keeping with the consumerist culture of late capitalism. He contrasts this with the revolutionary advent of Christianity in the ancient world, which was understandably attacked as "atheistic" for its assault upon "ten thousand immemorial cultic, social, and philosophical wisdoms." While he recognizes that the history of Christianity is at least in part the story of attempts to ignore or tame this original apocalyptic event, he maintains that it continues to*

*harbor an extraordinary destructive power, much more radi-
cal than the New Atheism, of which the more genuinely radical nihilistic atheisms are themselves only an offshoot.*

—JH

For charity's sake, we should avoid excessive kindness
here—or rather, I suppose, using the more appropriate
American cultural inflection, excessive niceness. There is no
need to take the small coterie of polemicists known collectively as the New Atheists particularly seriously, and I think
anyone more than passingly acquainted with the history of
ideas or the history of culture will recognize the defects of
their writings with little effort: the historical ignorance, the
casual misconceptions regarding what religious persons actually believe, the remarkable philosophical ineptitude with
which the claims of classical metaphysics are addressed
(even in books written by putatively trained philosophers),
the reflexively deistic or fundamentalist understanding of
God, the wanton slanders, the simplistic oppositions of
empty abstractions like "faith and reason," the absence of
any critical consciousness of the record of secular government, and so on. These are books written not for scholars,
but for a popular market where specialized knowledge
rarely intrudes with its tedious qualifications, corrections,
and inevitable ambiguities. True, morally speaking, any
scrupulous scholar is obliged to expend a certain quantity
of icy disdain upon the New Atheists for the extraordinary
violence they have committed against rational discourse on
belief and unbelief, the mystery of being, the meaning of
moral longing, and a host of other issues; but that is very

different from treating them with the respect due to the honorable, thoughtful atheists or skeptics of the past, or indeed of today. They occupy a place among unbelievers analogous to the place of modern fundamentalists among believers: they suffer from the same predispositions to ideological extremism, intellectual indolence, impatience with subtleties, simplistic mythologies, mindless rhetorical absolutism, and a very predictable authoritarianism (consider, for instance, how many of them have suggested that it should be illegal to raise one's children within one's faith, while never once taking Sam Harris to task for his fascist ruminations on the necessity of torture or of perhaps launching a nuclear first strike against the Muslim world).

This is, I acknowledge, a rather irascible way to open a sermon, but I can at least plead good intentions. My purpose is not really to abuse the New Atheists by rehearsing all the obvious complaints against them. I simply want to make a point about the spiritual sources of their incoherently, ferociously, but also very sincerely expressed discontent. It is my conviction, you see, that the sort of popular atheism to which they give voice, though it likes to represent itself as something daring and provocative and revolutionary, is in fact nothing of the kind; it is instead the rather banal final residue of the long history of capitalist modernity, and its chief impulse—as well as its chief moral deficiency—is bourgeois respectability. As a good Marxist might say, it is an ideological expression of the material conditions of its culture. Late modern industrial societies, whose economies are primarily consumerist, are already effectively atheist, insofar as the principal business of economic life in them has become the fabrication of an ever greater number of desires and the abolition of an ever greater number of the traditional prohibitions upon the gratification of those desires. Our sacred writ is advertising, our piety is shopping, our highest good is private choice. Late modern stories of personal and social liberation, at least for those enfolded in the warm and sheltering embrace of prosperous societies, are very frequently stories also about the shedding of all those limitations and inhibitions that might prevent us from being the perfect consumers our culture wishes us to be. In such a culture, the soul is something of an unpleasant encumbrance to have to carry about the shops with us, and God something of an inconvenient hindrance to the free play of our acquisitive longings, and both confront us with values that too often stand in stark rivalry to that one true source of value—the price tag—that occupies the moral center of our social world. So it really was only a matter of time before atheism descended from the ivory towers of academic and cosmopolitan fashion and began expressing itself in crassly popular form. The extraordinary intellectual vulgarity of the New Atheists is simply evidence that what once had to masquerade, even to itself, as a deep moral conviction and intense intellectual passion can now openly disport itself as the conventional and rather boring metaphysical rationality of a society shaped by the mechanisms and logic of the market. Nietzsche's aphoristic lightning bolts have been replaced by the insipid bromides of Richard Dawkins, who sells atheism as one might a line of Tupperware; the revolution ended long ago, and the vertiginous terror it once inspired of a dawning age of nihilism has now subsided into the calm complacency of a people whose chief moral labor is to avoid thinking too deeply about the violence or economic inequities upon which their material comforts rest. The appearance of the New Atheists is a phenomenon that was as inevitable as it is vapid.

All of which leads me to wonder whether the only true "atheism" ever to have appeared in the course of the evolution of Western civilization—that is, the only true form of "unbelief" that was also a real assault upon the God or gods of its age—was Christianity. Certainly, reflective intellectual historians have often enough noted the ironic continuity between the early modern rise of principled unbelief and the special "apocalyptic vocation" of Western culture; and the observations of Ernst Bloch and many others on the atheistic terminus of the Christian message are, if not exactly correct, at least intelligible: for modern Western atheism is chiefly a Christian heresy, and could not have arisen in a non-Christian setting. The New Atheism is merely an example of what happens when a new religious inspiration degenerates into an arid and infantile dogmatism, purged of historical memory and rational depth—when, that is, it ceases to inspire serious thought and begins to generate only therapies and catechisms. This is perhaps the most enchantingly naïve aspect of the New Atheism: that it mistakes its rather timorous and trite acquiescence to the spiritual prejudices and premises of its age for a struggle against a powerful tyranny, and its ignorance of the traditions it rejects for a bracingly principled critique of those traditions, and its submissive credence in a fairly threadbare positivism for some kind of intellectual and moral rebellion. You would think, though, that the New Atheists would have noticed by now that their views, far from reducing them to penury or driving them into catacombs or even causing a stir of scandal in polite society, have made them into well-remunerated celebrities cheerfully accepted by a popular culture that thrives only upon what it finds unthreatening and amusing. This should tell them something.

The "atheism" of the early Christians—an accusation quite justly leveled against them by their pagan critics—began in somewhat less comfortable conditions. In its earliest dawn, the gospel arrived in history as a kind of convulsive disruption *of* history, a subversive rejection of ten thousand immemorial cultic, social, and philosophical wisdoms (some of which it would later reclaim for itself, but only in altered form). And the event that the gospel proclaimed—the event within the event, so to speak—was the resurrection of Christ, which was not a religious event, nor an event within the history of religion, nor even a natural event, but a moment of pure interruption. According to Paul, it had effectively erased all sacred, social, racial, and national boundaries, destroying everything that separated peoples and classes from one another, subsuming into itself all divine sovereignty over history, and subduing all the spiritual agencies of the cosmos. It had placed the cosmic archons—the powers and principalities, the thrones and dominions, the "god of this world"—under Christ's foot. It was the event of a complete liberation from the constraints of elemental existence, one that even annulled the power of law—for the law, Paul said, even in its highest form, was still only delivered by an angel, through a human mediator, in order to act as a kind of probationary "disciplinarian" (*paid-agogos*), and had now been replaced by the law of love. The form in which Christianity entered human consciousness, that is to say, was not primarily a new system of practices and observances, or an alternative set of religious obligations, but first and foremost an apocalypse, the visionary annunciation of the Kingdom and its sudden invasion of historical time. It constituted an overturning of the logic of history and nature alike. It was an urgent command to all persons to come forth, out of the economies of society and cult, and into the immediacy of that event. Christianity was thus born in a terrible and joyous expectation of the eschatological—and yet already accomplished—abolition of the sacred: the abolition of, that is, the inviolable sacral divisions between peoples and classes, between the holy and the profane, between clean and unclean, between Jew and Gentile.

This meant, of course, that the early Christian community was not at first quite prepared to inhabit time except in a state of something like sustained crisis. There was no obvious medium by which a people in some sense already living in history's aftermath, in a state of constant urgency, could enter history again, as an institution, or an idea, or even a religion. In fact, as René Girard has often pointed out, the nature of the Christian apocalypse was, in a very profound sense, irreligious. It was a complete reversal of perspective in the realm of the sacred, an inversion of many of the holiest certitudes, the instant in which the victim of social and religious order—whom all human wisdom has always been prepared to hand over to death as a necessary and so legitimate sacrifice—was all at once seen as the righteous one, the innocent one, even God himself. At that moment, sacred order itself had fallen under judgment, and that hierarchy of human relations that religion serves, and in which it apportions all of us our proper places, had been exposed as nothing but an order of unjust violence, sustaining itself through ever more violence. From that revelation, once it had been even partially glimpsed, there could ultimately be no simple, innocent return to the violence of the sacred. From the beginning, consequently, there has been a certain paradoxical tension at the very heart of Christian belief and so of Christian culture. As a faith that began in rebellion against the limits and divisions produced in society and nature by the logic of the sacred, Christianity accords ill with almost any sort of cultic rationality. And, whereas a great many of the most venerable forms of religious practice constitute an attempt to affect a reconciliation between cosmic time and the time of spirit—by reintegrating human beings into the cycle of the seasons, say, or of life and death—the first "waking moment" of the gospel came with a pressing awareness of the nearness of the end, and a knowledge that cosmic redemption must come in the form of judgment. It would take some time, and some degree of adjustment of expectations, and perhaps even a considerable degree of disenchantment, for so singular an irruption of the eschatological into the temporal to be recuperated into stable order again.

Inevitably, though, it had to be. A purely apocalyptic consciousness—a consciousness subsisting solely in a moment of pure interruption—cannot really be sustained beyond a certain very brief period. The exigencies of sheer material existence demanded that Christianity would in time have to become "historical" again, "cultural" again, which is to say, "cultic." What began primarily as force could not endure except as structure; the event had to crystallize into something that could persist within history. It is not surprising, therefore, that Christianity took on a religious shape conformable to its environment, incorporating practices and language intelligible to the religious imaginations of ancient men and women, even as it strove to generate new kinds of community within the shelter of the form it had assumed. And, naturally, as is inevitably the case whenever historical necessity becomes a determining element within any story, the results of this accommodation between apocalypse and cult were very frequently tragic. As a religion, Christianity has provided many guises by which the original provocation of the Christian event has been made more bearable to historical consciousness, but under which it has far too often been all but entirely hidden. The religious impulse has served as the necessary vehicle by which an essentially apocalyptic awareness has been conveyed through the alien element of "fallen" time, but has also frequently acted as a rival to that awareness.

The alloy, moreover, has probably always been a somewhat unstable one. The Christian event is of its nature something too refractory and volatile—the impulse to rebellion too constitutive of its own spiritual logic—to be contained even within its own institutions. This is why Christianity over the centuries not only has proved so irrepressibly fissile, as all large religious traditions to some degree are, but has also given rise to a culture capable of the most militant atheism, and even of self-conscious nihilism (modern Western atheism, again, being only a kind of heretical Christian messianism). As essentially an interruption, Christianity's power of creativity has always been closely allied to its power of destruction, and so probably can never come fully to rest in any stable cultural forms, even those it has generated. Even in its most enduring and necessary historical configurations, there persists within it an ungovernable energy, something that desires not to crystallize but to disperse itself into the future, to start always anew, more spirit than flesh or letter.

Compared to that original revolutionary moment, that first and (I suspect) unique moment of rebellion against sacred order and religious "truth," and seen within the context of the irrepressible spiritual ferment that it released into the historical consciousness of the West, the New Atheism really does often look like nothing more than a somewhat belated reactionary attempt to subdue the anarchic forces of the apocalyptic once and for all—to chase away those terrible visions of judgment and replace them at last with the bright, diversionary spectacle of a comfortable consumerist secularity. In this sense, the banality of the New Atheism may be the deepest source of its appeal; it is, in the end, a form of narcotic. And, in its defense, what it offers is far less confusing and troubling than what it seeks to displace. Christianity from the beginning understood itself not simply as a timeless wisdom revealed, but as a dynamic invasion of time by eternity, a particular history that altered the frame of things, not only on earth, but in the heavens as well. It is that event that issues a call, in any generation, to those disposed to hear it, and even to those who are not. But it is also an event that remains always somewhat incomprehensible within the limits of time as we experience it—an event whose proclamation we have always yet to understand.

Bibliography

Baker, Lynne Rudder. "Cognitive Suicide." In *Contents of Thought*, edited by Robert H. Grimm and Daniel Davy Merrill, 1–18. Tucson: University of Arizona Press, 1988.

Beattie, Tina. *The New Atheists: The Twilight of Reason and the War on Religion*. London: Darton, Longman & Todd, 2007.

Bitbol, Michel. "Materialism, Stances and Open-Mindedness." In *Images of Empiricism: Essays on Science and Stances, with a Reply from Bas van Fraassen*, edited by Bradley Monton, 229–70. Oxford: Oxford University Press, 2007.

Buss, Leo W. *The Evolution of Individuality*. Princeton: Princeton University Press, 1987.

Chesterton, G. K. *Orthodoxy*. London: Fontana, 1961.

Cornwell, John. *Darwin's Angel: An Angelic Riposte to* The God Delusion. London: Profile, 2007.

Cornwell, John, and Michael McGhee, editors. *Philosophers and God: At the Frontiers of Faith and Reason*. London: Continuum, 2009.

Cunningham, Conor. *Darwin's Pious Idea: Why the Ultra-Darwinists and Creationists Both Get it Wrong*. Grand Rapids: Eerdmans, 2010.

———. *Genealogy of Nihilism*. London: Routledge, 2002.

Davison, Andrew, editor. *Imaginative Apologetics: Theology, Philosophy, and the Catholic Tradition* London: SCM, 2011.

Dawkins, Richard. *A Devil's Chaplain: Selected Essays by Richard Dawkins*. London: Weidenfield & Nicholson, 2003.

———. *The God Delusion*. London: Bantam, 2006.

Dooley, Gillian, editor. *From a Tiny Corner in the House of Fiction: Conversations with Iris Murdoch*. Columbia: University of South Carolina Press, 2003.

Bibliography

Dostoyevsky, Fyodor. *The Brothers Karamazov*. London: Penguin, 1993.

Eagleton, Terry. *Reason, Faith, and Revolution: Reflections on the God Debate*. New Haven: Yale University Press, 2010.

Fergusson, David. *Faith and Its Critics: A Conversation*. Oxford: Oxford University Press, 2011.

Fodor, Jerry. "Is Science Biologically Possible?" In *Naturalism Defeated? Essays on Plantinga's Evolutionary Argument against Naturalism*, edited by James Beilby, 30–42. Ithaca: Cornell University Press, 2002.

Fontana, Walter. "The Typology of the Possible." In *Understanding Change: Models, Methodologies, and Metaphors*, edited by Andreas Wimmer and Reinhart Kössler. Basingstoke: Palgrave Macmillan, 2005.

Fontana, Walter, and Leo W. Buss. "The Arrival of the Fittest: Toward a Theory of Biological Organization." *Bulletin of Mathematical Biology* 56 (1994) 1–64.

Ghiselin, Michael. *Metaphysics and the Origin of Species*. Albany: State University of New York Press, 1997.

Hart, David Bentley. *Atheist Delusions: The Christian Revolution and Its Fashionable Enemies*. New Haven: Yale University Press, 2010.

———. *The Doors of the Sea: Where Was God in the Tsunami?* Grand Rapids: Eerdmanns, 2005.

Hughes, John. *The End of Work: Theological Critiques of Captialism*. Oxford: Blackwell, 2007.

Hutchinson, George Evelyn. "The Ecological Theater and the Evolutionary Play." In *The Ecological Theatre and the Evolutionary Play*. New Haven: Yale University Press, 1965.

Jacob, François. *The Logic of Life: A History of Heredity*. Translated by Betty Spillman. New York: Pantheon, 1973.

Jenkins, Timothy. *An Experiment in Providence: How Faith Engages the World*. London: SPCK, 2006.

———. *Religion in English Everyday Life: An Ethnographic Approach*. New York: Berghahn, 1999.

Jonas, Hans. *The Phenomenon of Life: Toward a Philosophical Biology*. Evanston: Northwestern University Press, 2001.

Kahane, Ernest. *La vie n'existe pas!* Paris: Éditions Rationalistes, 1962.

Koslowski, Peter. "The Theory of Evolution as Sociobiology and Bioeconomics: A Critique of Its Claim to Totality." In *Sociobiology and Bioeconomics: The Theory of Evolution in Biological and Economic Theory*, edited by Peter Koslowski, 301–28. Berlin: Springer, 1998.

Lash, Nicholas. *The Beginning and End of "Religion."* Cambridge: Cambridge University Press, 1996.

Le Fanu, James. *Why Us? How Science Rediscovered the Mystery of Ourselves.* New York: Pantheon, 2009.

Lewontin, Richard. "Billions and Billions of Demons." Review of *The Demon-Haunted World: Science as a Candle in the Dark,* by Carl Sagan. *New York Review of Books,* January 9th, 1997, 28–32.

Lubac, Henri de. *The Drama of Atheist Humanism.* Translated by Edith M. Riley, Anne Englund Nash, and Mark Sebanc. San Francisco: Ignatius, 1995.

MacIntyre, Alasdair. *After Virtue: A Study in Moral Theory.* London: Duckworth, 1981.

———. *Whose Justice? Which Rationality?* London: Duckworth, 1996.

Markusson, Gudmundur. Review of *The God Delusion,* by Richard Dawkins. *Journal of Cognition and Culture* 7 (2007) 369–73.

McGrath, Alister. *Dawkins' God: Genes, Memes, and the Meaning of Life.* Oxford: Blackwell, 2005.

———. *Why God Won't Go Away: Engaging with the New Atheism.* London: SPCK, 2011.

McGrath, Alister, and Joanna Collicut McGrath. *The Dawkins Delusion: Atheist Fundamentalism and the Denial of the Divine.* London: SPCK, 2007.

Metzinger, Thomas. *Being No One: The Self-Model Theory of Subjectivity.* Cambridge: MIT Press, 2003.

Michod, Richard E. "Cooperation and Conflict in the Evolution of Individuality." *American Naturalist* 149:4 (1997) 607–45.

———. *Darwinian Dynamics: Evolutionary Transitions in Fitness and Individuality.* Princeton: Princeton University Press, 1999.

Newman, John Henry. *The Letters and Diaries of John Henry Newman.* 32 vols. Edited by Ian Ker et al. Oxford: Clarendon, 1961.

O'Hear, Anthony. *Beyond Evolution: Human Nature and the Limits of Evolutionary Explanation.* Oxford: Oxford University Press, 1997.

Popper, Karl, and John C. Eccles. *The Self and Its Brain: An Argument for Interactionism.* Berlin: Springer, 1977.

Quine, Willard Van Orman. "Two Dogmas of Empiricism." In *From a Logical Point of View: Nine Logico-Philosophical Essays,* 20–46. New York: Harper & Row, 1951.

Ratzinger, Joseph Cardinal. *Truth and Tolerance: Christian Belief and World Religions.* San Francisco: Ignatius, 2004.

Ruse, Michael, and Edward O. Wilson. "The Evolution of Ethics." In *Religion and the Natural Sciences: The Range of Engagement,* edited by James Huchingson, 308–27. Fort Worth: Harcourt Brace Jovanovich, 1993.

Russell, Bertrand. *An Outline of Philosophy*. London: Routledge, 1927.

Schloss, Jeffrey P. "Would Venus Evolve on Mars? Bioenergetic Constraints, Allometric Trends, and the Evolution of Life-History Invariants." In *Fitness of the Cosmos for Life: Biochemistry and Fine-Tuning*, edited by John Barrow et al., 318–46. Cambridge: Cambridge University Press, 2008.

Seager, William. "Real Patterns and Surface Metaphysics." In *Dennett's Philosophy: A Comprehensive Assessment*, edited by Don Ross, Andrew Brook, and David Thompson, 95–129. Cambridge: MIT Press, 2000.

Searle, John. *The Mystery of Consciousness*. London: Granta, 1997.

Shostak, Stanley. *Death of Life: The Legacy of Molecular Biology*. London: Macmillan, 1998.

Snow, C. P. *The Two Cultures*. Cambridge: Cambridge University Press, 1993.

Steiner, George. *Real Presences: Is There Anything in What We Say?* London: Faber, 1991.

Stich, Stephen. *Deconstructing the Mind*. Oxford: Oxford University Press, 1996.

Stroud, Barry. "The Charm of Naturalism." *Proceedings and Addresses of the American Philosophical Association* 70:2 (1996) 43–55.

Tomalin, Nicholas. *Nicholas Tomalin Reporting*. London: Deutsch, 1975.

Van Fraassen, Bas C. *The Empirical Stance*. New Haven: Yale University Press, 2002.

———. "Science, Materialism, and False Consciousness." In *Warrant in Contemporary Epistemology: Essays in Honor of Plantinga's Theory of Knowledge*, edited by Jonathan Kvanvig, 149–81. Lanham: Rowman & Littlefield, 1996.

Wallace, Alan. *The Taboo of Subjectivity: Toward a New Science of Consciousness*. Oxford: Oxford University Press, 2000.

Contributors

Tina Beattie is professor of Catholic Studies and Director of the Digby Stuart Research Centre at the University of Roehampton. She is the author of *God's Mother, Eve's Advocate* (Continuum, 2002), *New Catholic Feminism: Theology and Theory* (Routledge, 2006), and *The New Atheists* (Darton, Longman, & Todd, 2007).

John Cornwell is the Director of the Science and Human Dimension Project and a Fellow Commoner at Jesus College. In addition to a career in journalism, he is the author of many books including *Hitler's Pope* (Penguin, 2000), *Darwin's Angel* (Profile, 2008), and *Newman's Unquiet Grave* (Continuum, 2011). He is also the co-editor with Michael McGhee of *Philosophers and God* (Continuum, 2009).

Conor Cunningham is a Lecturer in Theology and Religious Studies and Co-Director of the Centre of Theology and Philosophy at the University of Nottingham. He is the author of *Genealogy of Nihilism* (Routledge, 2002) and *Darwin's Pious Idea* (Eerdmans, 2010), as well as many other chapters and articles.

Terry Eagleton is currently Distinguished Professor of English Literature at Lancaster University, Professor of

Cultural Theory at the National University of Ireland, and Distinguished Visiting Professor of English Literature at the University of Notre Dame. He has previously taught at the Universities of Oxford and Manchester and is a Fellow of the British Academy and an Honorary Fellow of Jesus College, Cambridge. His many publications include: *The Ideology of the Aesthetic* (Wiley-Blackwell, 1990), *Literary Theory* (University of Minnesota Press, 2008), *The Illusions of Postmodernism* (Blackwell, 1996), *After Theory* (Penguin, 2004), *Reason, Faith and Revolution* (Yale University Press, 2010), *On Evil* (Yale University Press, 2011), and *Why Marx was Right* (Yale University Press, 2011).

David Fergusson is Professor of Divinity at New College in the University of Edinburgh and a minister in the Church of Scotland. His books include *Community, Liberalism and Christian Ethics* (Cambridge University Press, 1998), *Church, State, and Civil Society* (Cambridge University Press, 2004), and *Faith and its Critics* (Oxford University Press, 2009). He has given the Bampton, Gifford, and Warfield lectures and is a Fellow of the Royal Society of Edinburgh.

David Bentley Hart is an Eastern Orthodox Theologian who has taught theology at the University of Virginia, the University of St. Thomas (Minnesota), Duke Divinity School, and Loyola College (Maryland). He held the Robert J. Randall Chair in Christian Culture at Providence College. His books include *The Beauty of the Infinite* (Eerdmans, 2003), *The Doors of the Sea* (Eerdmans, 2005), *The Story of Christianity* (Quercus, 2007), and *Atheist Delusions* (Yale University Press, 2009), which received the 2011 Michael Ramsey Prize in Theology.

John Hughes is a Fellow and Dean of Chapel at Jesus College, Cambridge. He was ordained priest in the Diocese of Exeter and now teaches philosophy and ethics for the University of Cambridge Faculty of Divinity. He is the author of *The End of Work: Theological Critiques of Capitalism* (Blackwell, 2009) and various chapters and articles.

Timothy Jenkins is Reader in Anthropology and Religion in the University of Cambridge Faculty of Divinity and a Fellow of Jesus College. He is a priest in the Church of England and his publications include *Religion in Everyday English Life* (Berghahn, 1999), and *An Experiment in Providence* (SPCK, 2006), in addition to various articles on European social anthropology and ethnography.

Alister McGrath is a theologian and priest who is now Professor of Theology, Ministry, and Education at King's College London and Head of the Centre for Theology, Religion and Culture. He was previously Professor of Historical Theology and Principal of Wycliffe Hall in the University of Oxford. He has published widely in historical academic theology as well as more popular apologetics, including *The Twilight of Atheism* (Doubleday, 2004), *Dawkin's God* (Blackwell, 2004), *The Dawkins Delusion?* (SPCK, 2007), and *Why God Won't Go Away* (SPCK, 2011). He has given the Bampton and Hulsean lectures, the latter published as *Darwinism and the Divine* (Blackwell-Wiley, 2011).

Index

Index

Index

THE — POTATO COOKBOOK

Varieties text supplied by
the Potato Marketing Board

THE
POTATO
COOKBOOK

EDITED BY
NICOLA HILL

Mitchell Beazley

First published in Great Britain in 1994
by Mitchell Beazley
an imprint of Reed Consumer Books Limited
Michelin House, 81 Fulham Road, London SW3 6RB
and Auckland, Melbourne, Singapore and Toronto

Reprinted 1995

ISBN 1 85732 413 7

A CIP catalogue record for this book is available from
the British Library

Printed in Singapore

Acknowledgements

Art Director: Jacqui Small
Art Editors: Meryl James & Sue Michniewicz
Commissioning Editor: Nicola Hill
Editors: Isobel Holland & Jo Lethaby
Production Controller: Sasha Judelson
Jacket Photographer: Nick Carman
Photographer: Alan Newnham
Home Economist: Jennie Shapter
Stylist: Jane McLeish
Illustrator: Roger Kent/Garden Studios

Notes

Both metric and imperial measurements have been
given in all recipes. Use one set of measurements only
and not a mixture of both.

Standard level spoon measurements are used in all
recipes.
1 tablespoon = one 15 ml spoon
1 teaspoon = one 5 ml spoon

Eggs should be size 3 unless otherwise stated.

Milk should be full fat unless otherwise stated.

Ovens should be preheated to the specified temperature
– if using a fan assisted oven, follow the manufacturer's
instructions for adjusting the time and the temperature.

The potato must be one of the most widely eaten vegetables in the world, although mostly in just one of its manifestations, the French fry or chip. Despite the disproportionate fame of this single form of preparation, potatoes are one of the most versatile of vegetables and have been a staple in both hemispheres, across the continents and centuries. Not only that, but they can appear in any course of a meal – from the hors d'oeuvres and soups, through to main courses either as an accompaniment or as the main dish, to cakes and puddings.

Although it was, for a time, vilified as being 'fattening' and was excluded from the plates of the figure-conscious, a more complete understanding of nutrition has led to the potato being rehabilitated, as long as the temptation to add butter is avoided! Potatoes are not just tasty, they are actually good for you and provide a valuable source of easily digested starch, vitamin C, protein, potassium, iron, thiamin, niacin and dietary fibre, while containing no fat or cholesterol.

Growth Habit For gardeners in temperate areas potatoes are conveniently divided according to the season in which they mature and are therefore categorized as first earlies, second earlies and maincrop. First earlies tend to be waxy, simply because their moisture content is high. The same variety, if left to mature fully, may present quite different cooking qualities. There are waxy and floury types in the later categories, although the soil and season have an effect.

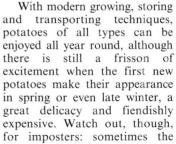

With modern growing, storing and transporting techniques, potatoes of all types can be enjoyed all year round, although there is still a frisson of excitement when the first new potatoes make their appearance in spring or even late winter, a great delicacy and fiendishly expensive. Watch out, though, for imposters: sometimes the very first 'news' to appear are simply underage maincrop varieties and are never as tasty as the proper new varieties.

Nothing compares, however, with lifting your own potatoes, to be eaten within half an hour. However, it is certainly more work than going to the shops, but keen gardeners can provide a year round supply of high-quality potatoes with some ingenuity, favourable weather conditions, careful storage and freedom from disease.

FIRST EARLIES

These small, immature potatoes are a great treat in spring and early summer and are known for their delicate and sweet flavour. The skins should come away readily when rubbed gently. They are all suitable for steaming, boiling and are a great asset in salads. They are normally available from May onwards and are grown in areas which favour quick growth and are generally not prone to late frosts.

Arran Pilot
This is recommended for light soils. The attractive, kidney-shaped tubers have white, firm flesh and are produced in quantity. These potatoes are excellent in salads and can be suitable for baking and making delicious chips.

Duke of York
A kidney-shaped potato with yellow flesh. It performs well on most soils, even heavy ones, and has an excellent flavour. As well as being a heavy cropper, it is suitable for forcing.

Elvira
An Italian early with a creamy-coloured skin and flesh, it is ideal for using in salads either steamed or lightly boiled. Best served in its skin as this helps to retain the flavour.

Epicure
Known for its old-fashioned flavour and hardiness in cold conditions. The tubers are round with deep eyes. An excellent hardy variety and a prolific cropper. Makes very good mashed potatoes, but can also be boiled and used in salads.

Epicure

Home Guard
This rather short, oval potato has white skin and white flesh, which has a tendency to be slightly floury when cooked, and is best fried or boiled. This variety does not do well in dry soil conditions.

Home Guard

Maris Bard
Oval tubers of medium size with white skin and shallow eyes. The white flesh is firm and moist in texture and does not blacken on cooking. The taste is delicate and most suited to boiling and also for use in salads.

Pentland Javlin
These short, oval tubers have very smooth white skin and shallow eyes. Boiling is a particularly suitable use for this waxy, white-fleshed early variety.

Rocket
The tubers of this white-skinned variety are round, and medium to large in size. The white flesh is firm and waxy with a good flavour and does not blacken after cooking. Again, boiling and salads are the best uses for this potato.

Vanessa
This is a particularly versatile first early. It has an attractive pink skin colour with a light

Vanessa

yellow flesh and a delicious flavour. It is slightly waxy when cooked and is, therefore, very good served either plain boiled or steamed.

SECOND EARLIES

Larger than the first earlies, because they spend longer in the ground, second earlies bridge the gap between new potatoes and maincrops. They are available between August and March.

Ausonia
This variety is of Dutch origin. It has a light yellow skin and flesh with a slightly waxy texture, which makes this potato most suitable for either boiling or steaming.

Catriona
This has a pale yellow skin with red-coloured eyes and cream-

Catriona

coloured flesh and it has a good flavour. As it has a slightly floury texture it is ideal for making good roast potatoes. However, it does just as well either baked or steamed.

Estima
A good all-rounder, but perhaps best for baking. The plump, oval tubers have a smooth, light yellow skin and flesh that is moist and firm. It is one of the earliest potatoes of the year that can be baked satisfactorily. Other uses are boiling and chipping.

Great Scot
An old variety, with a high yield of round tubers that store very well. It is a great favourite for baking.

Marfona
A robust variety which survives well on poor soil. The plant produces large tubers with white flesh which are noted for baking. These potatoes can also be boiled but are not suitable for roasting.

Maris Peer
A short, oval tuber with shallow eyes. The skin and flesh are white. This potato has an excellent flavour and is best

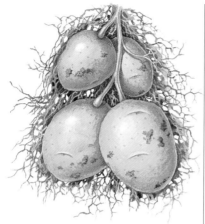

Maris Peer

when served either plain boiled or steamed.

Nadine

A new variety which was raised in Scotland, these tubers are round to oval in shape and have a firm and waxy flesh, which makes them ideal for use in salads and either boiling or steaming.

Royal Kidney (Jersey New)

Oval-shaped tuber with a yellow skin and light yellow flesh which is soft rather than firm. They are best served whole in their skins either plain boiled or steamed.

Wilja

A reliable and heavy yielding variety. The tubers are elongated-oval or sometimes pear-shaped, and both skin and flesh are yellow. The flesh is firm, with a good flavour but can be on the dry side, making it most suitable for boiling, baking and mashing.

Wilja

COOKING FOR QUALITY

A renewal of interest in less usual varieties has provided the stimulus to supermarket chains that now supply 'heritage' potatoes, albeit at a price. Simply knowing which is the most suitable type for the culinary purpose you have in mind, and using them accordingly, makes all the difference – good baking potatoes and mashing potatoes, for example, can't be expected to perform well in salads. By keeping in mind a short list of varieties when you go shopping, or looking up any new varities you come across will soon increase your knowedge of what potato to buy for your particular requirements.

Despite the variety of potatoes available, at least in theory, they can be divided into just two categories according to their cooking qualities – waxy and floury or mealy.

Waxy potatoes have a relatively low starch content, but considerable moisture and thin skins. They hold their shape well when boiled or steamed and are excellent cold in salads or served hot and whole with just a little butter. Floury potatoes have more starch and become fluffy and light when cooked. They perform best as bakers or for mashing, but may fall apart if boiled for too long. This, of course, can be an advantage in thickening soups. Both types can be successfully deep-fried.

MAINCROP

These are sometimes referred to as 'old' potatoes, even when they are newly lifted. Since they are allowed to mature and bulk up on the plant, the tubers are usually large. They are generally available between September and May.

Bintje
This variety produces oval to long-shaped tubers which have shallow eyes. The skin is pale yellow and the flesh is a light, creamy yellow. It is suitable for all cooking methods, but particularly good for making chips.

Cara
The large round tubers are easily recognized by their white skins which are parti-coloured pink around the eyes. The cream flesh has a soft, moist texture making it excellent for baking. Cara can also be used successfully for boiling and chipping.

Desirée
A red-skinned variety with medium depth eyes. Tubers are large ovals with light yellow, firm flesh which has good all-round cooking qualities. Desirée potatoes are recommended for roasting, boiling, chipping and baking.

Golden Wonder
These are long oval-shaped tubers with medium-depth eyes, the skin is dark russet in colour and the flesh is light yellow. It has rather lost out to other varieties, but used to be most highly regarded. It is a potato best used for baking but can be good for mashed potatoes or used in salads.

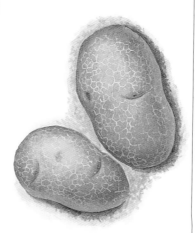

Golden Wonder

Kerr's Pink
These are rounded tubers with a markedly pink skin and creamy flesh. The texture of the flesh is floury. It is suitable for most types of cooking but not very good in salads.

Kerr's Pink

King Edward
One of the best known and best-loved of the British varieties. The tubers are small and oval with parti-coloured pink and white skin. The flesh of this high quality potato is creamy white and has a floury texture and rarely discolours on cooking. Best uses are mashing, roasting, chipping and baking. It is not recommended for use in salads.

Kingston
A relative newcomer, introduced in 1981, these oval tubers have a pale yellow skin and flesh with a waxy texture when cooked. Excellent for boiling.

Maris Piper
This is the most widely used British variety. The short oval tubers have a pale cream-coloured skin and a creamy white flesh with a pleasant floury texture. A good all round potato, Maris Piper can be used for boiling, baking, chipping and roasting, however, it is not to be recommended for use in salads.

Pentland Dell
These shallow eyed, long oval tubers have white skin and a pale creamy white flesh, but not a strong flavour. The texture is moderately soft and dry and has a tendency to break up on boiling.

Pentland Squire
A good all round variety, the Pentland Squire has a white skin, which is occasionally russetted, with medium depth eyes. The mild flavour of this variety's white flesh and its soft, floury texture is most suited to mashing, roasting or baking.

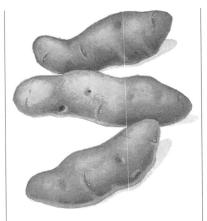

Pink Fir Apple

Pink Fir Apple
This is still a relative curiosity as it was only introduced in 1979. It has knobbly, elongated tubers and pink skin that can be awkward to peel. Good growing conditions produce smoother results. It also tends to keep rather well. The strongly flavoured flesh is yellow with a firm, waxy texture, and is excellent in salads, it can also be a useful addition to stews and casseroles or alternatively simply plain boiled.

Ratte
Another less usual variety, which is widely grown in France. The tubers are smallish and elongated and are waxy when cooked, giving excellent results in salads, from the point of view of both texture and flavour.

Romano
Another red-skinned variety with large oval tubers and cream-coloured flesh. It has a fairly firm texture with a slight susceptibility to blackening after cooking. Not a particularly exciting flavour, but it is a good all round cooking potato particularly suited for either mashing, boiling, roasting or baking.

Romano

Roseval

A particular favourite with the French, this tuber with its red skin and yellow flesh has an extremely good flavour and an excellent texture when cooked. It is best suited to boiling or steaming and can therefore be used in salads. It is also good to fry.

Roseval

Shelagh

A Scottish variety which has a parti-coloured skin with a pinkish tinge to the eyes. The flesh is creamy coloured with a waxy texture, making it ideal for either boiling or steaming.

Shelagh

BUYING AND STORING POTATOES

Select tubers that are firm and heavy with no obvious soft spots and no visible green or black discoloured patches, and make sure the skin is tight. Potatoes that have started to sprout from the eyes should be discarded instantly.

Although it is tempting and often cheaper to buy potatoes in bulk or large quantities, do resist buying more at a time than you can consume in about 2-3 weeks, unless you have the ideal storage conditions.

Store potatoes in cool, dark and dry conditions. Earlies and new potatoes are always better used as soon as possible after lifting and cannot be stored for any length of time. Maincrop potatoes, however, can be kept until the first new potatoes are ready for harvest, with the proviso that any damaged or diseased tubers must be discarded promptly.

Other useful points to bear in mind when purchasing – the skin of new potatoes should rub away with gentle finger pressure, in fact it should be flaking off; most potatoes are bought in plastic bags at supermarkets, transfer to a paper bag or wrap in newspaper when storing as they will keep in a much better condition and for much longer; ready-washed potatoes do not store as well or for as long as earthy ones and should be eaten as soon after the day of purchase as possible; finally, do not store potatoes in a refrigerator as low temperatures set up a chemical reaction resulting in discoloured, green flesh.

POTATO & CELERY SOUP

Serves 4

25 g (*1 oz*) butter
½ head celery, cut into 2.5 cm (*1 inch*) pieces
2 onions, chopped
500 g (*1 lb*) potatoes, peeled and quartered
600 ml (*1 pint*) chicken or vegetable stock
250 ml (*8 fl oz*) milk
50-75 g (*2-3 oz*) Double Gloucester cheese, grated
salt and freshly ground black pepper

Melt the butter in a saucepan, add the celery and onions, and cook gently without browning. Add the potatoes and stock with salt and pepper to taste. Bring to the boil, reduce the heat and simmer for about 20 minutes until all the vegetables are tender.

Purée in a liquidizer or food processor, or rub through a sieve. Return the soup to the rinsed pan. Add the milk, reheat and adjust the seasoning. Serve very hot, sprinkled with the grated cheese.

CHILLED BASIL & POTATO SOUP

Serves 4

15 g (*½ oz*) butter
750 g (*1½ lb*) floury potatoes, peeled and grated
6 garlic cloves, halved
50 g (*2 oz*) fresh basil, chopped
750 ml (*1¼ pints*) chicken stock
600 ml (*1 pint*) dry white wine
1 teaspoon lemon juice
15 g (*½ oz*) pine nuts, ground
salt and freshly ground black pepper

Melt the butter in a large heavy-based saucepan and add the potatoes, garlic and half the basil. Stir over a gentle heat for a couple of minutes, then add the stock and wine.

Bring to the boil and cook uncovered for 15 minutes, until the potatoes are soft. Purée with the remaining basil in a liquidizer or food processor, or rub through a sieve into a bowl. Add lemon juice, salt and pepper to taste, remembering that since the soup is to be served chilled the seasoning will need to be a little more pronounced.

Mix the ground pine nuts with 2 tablespoons of the soup in a small bowl. Stir the mixture into the soup. Chill thoroughly before serving.

Illustrated opposite

POTATO & CIDER SOUP

Serves 5-6

250 g (*8 oz*) onions, sliced
500 g (*1 lb*) cooking apples,
peeled, cored and sliced
1 kg (*2 lb*) potatoes, peeled and sliced
300 ml (*½ pint*) cider
1.2 litres (*2 pints*) vegetable stock
1 teaspoon dried mixed herbs
1 teaspoon ground coriander
150 ml (*¼ pint*) natural yogurt
salt and freshly ground black pepper
snipped fresh chives, or chopped fresh mint,
to garnish

Combine the onions, apples and potatoes in a saucepan and add the cider. Bring to the boil and cook briskly for 10 minutes, stirring from time to time. Add the stock, dried herbs and coriander. Cover the pan and simmer the soup for about 25 minutes, until all the vegetables are very tender.

Purée the soup in a liquidizer or food processor, or rub through a coarse sieve. Return to the rinsed pan and stir in the yogurt, reserving 1 tablespoon for garnish. Season with salt and pepper and reheat. Serve with a little yogurt swirled into each bowl and sprinkled with fresh chives or mint.

SWEETCORN & POTATO CHOWDER

Serves 4

125 g (*4 oz*) smoked haddock
150 ml (*¼ pint*) milk
25 g (*1 oz*) butter
125 g (*4 oz*) rindless streaky bacon, diced
500 g (*1 lb*) potatoes, peeled and diced
1 large onion, chopped
375 g (*12 oz*) can sweetcorn
600 ml (*1 pint*) chicken stock
150 ml (*¼ pint*) single cream
1 tablespoon chopped fresh parsley
salt and freshly ground black pepper

Place the haddock in a saucepan with the milk. Simmer for 10 minutes or until the fish flakes easily when tested with the point of a knife. Remove the fish with a slotted spoon and place on a board. Remove the skin and bones, flake the fish and set it aside. Reserve the cooking liquid in a jug.

Melt the butter in a large saucepan, add the bacon and fry over a moderately high heat until golden. Add the potatoes and onion, cover the pan, reduce the heat and cook slowly until the onion is soft but not browned.

Add the sweetcorn, stock, flaked fish and reserved cooking liquid. Simmer gently for 10-15 minutes. Stir in the cream and parsley and season to taste with salt and pepper.

POTATO & TUNA SALAD

Serves 4-6

500 g (*1 lb*) potatoes, scrubbed
250 g (*8 oz*) drained canned tuna,
coarsely flaked
50 g (*2 oz*) button mushrooms, sliced
1 red onion, thinly sliced in rings

DRESSING:

125 ml (*4 fl oz*) natural yogurt
grated rind and juice of ½ lemon
1 tablespoon chopped fresh parsley
salt and freshly ground black pepper

Cook the potatoes in a saucepan of lightly
salted boiling water until just tender. Drain
well. Let the potatoes cool, then slice them
thickly into a salad bowl.

Add the flaked tuna, sliced mushrooms and
red onion rings to the potatoes.

For the dressing, mix the yogurt with the
lemon rind and juice. Stir in the chopped
parsley with salt and pepper to taste. Pour the
dressing over the salad and toss lightly.

NEW POTATO, CHESHIRE CHEESE & CASHEW NUT SALAD

Serves 6-8

750 g (*1½ lb*) new potatoes, scrubbed
6 tablespoons French dressing
4 spring onions, sliced,
or 2 tablespoons snipped fresh chives
125 g (*4 oz*) Cheshire cheese, finely diced
75 g (*3 oz*) salted cashew nuts
12-16 tiny cherry tomatoes
salt and freshly ground black pepper

Cook the potatoes in a saucepan of lightly
salted boiling water for about 10-15 minutes
until they are all just tender. Drain them and
roughly dice.

Place the potatoes in a bowl and while they
are still hot, add the French dressing. Mix
well, add the spring onions or chives, then
cover and leave to cool.

Add the cheese, cashew nuts and cherry
tomatoes, season well with salt and pepper
and mix lightly. Serve at once or chill in a
covered bowl until required.

CALIFORNIAN POTATO SALAD

Serves 4-6

750 g (*1½ lb*) small new potatoes, scrubbed
125 g (*4 oz*) rindless streaky bacon
125 g (*4 oz*) raisins
25 g (*1 oz*) cashew nuts

DRESSING:

4 tablespoons natural yogurt
1 teaspoon clear honey
50 g (*2 oz*) blue cheese, grated
salt and freshly ground black pepper

Boil or steam the new potatoes until tender, about 15-20 minutes, depending upon size. Drain thoroughly, place in a bowl and allow to cool, if liked.

Grill the bacon until crisp, then crumble or chop coarsely. Mix the bacon with the potatoes and add the raisins.

To make the dressing, mix the yogurt with the honey and cheese in a bowl. Add salt and pepper to taste. Add to the potato mixture and toss well to coat.

Serve the salad warm or cold, sprinkled with the cashew nuts.

POTATO SALAD WITH SALMON & PRAWNS

Serves 4

625 g (*1¼ lb*) waxy potatoes, scrubbed
50 g (*2 oz*) smoked salmon, cut into thin strips
250 g (*8 oz*) cooked peeled prawns
125g (*4 oz*) seedless white grapes, halved
50 g (*2 oz*) pecan nuts
1 tablespoon snipped fresh chives
1 tablespoon chopped fresh dill, to garnish

DRESSING:

2 tablespoons mayonnaise
4 tablespoons soured cream
1 tablespoon lemon juice
salt and freshly ground black pepper

Cook the potatoes in a saucepan of lightly salted boiling water for 15-20 minutes until just tender. Drain well. When cool, slice the potatoes into a salad bowl.

Add the smoked salmon, prawns, grapes, pecan nuts and snipped chives. Mix the salad lightly, using two forks.

For the dressing, mix all the ingredients in a small bowl. Whisk until thoroughly combined. Pour the dressing over the salad. Toss lightly to coat, sprinkle with dill and serve.

Illustrated opposite

16

PEANUT POTATO SALAD

Serves 4

500 g (*1 lb*) new potatoes, scrubbed
50 g (*2 oz*) thickly sliced cooked ham, diced
4 tablespoons mayonnaise
1 tablespoon peanut butter
lettuce leaves
50 g (*2 oz*) salted peanuts

Boil or steam the new potatoes until tender, about 15-20 minutes, depending upon size. Drain if necessary.

Place the potatoes in a bowl. Add the ham and mix lightly. Mix the mayonnaise and peanut butter together in a small bowl; add to the potato mixture and stir lightly.

Arrange the lettuce leaves on a serving plate and spoon the potato mixture on top. Sprinkle with the salted peanuts.

SPANISH POTATO SALAD

Serves 4

500 g (*1 lb*) new potatoes, scrubbed, or larger
potatoes, peeled and cut into bite-sized pieces
salt
DRESSING:
3 tablespoons tomato purée
3 tablespoons olive oil
1 tablespoon lemon juice
1 garlic clove, crushed
few drops of Tabasco or chilli sauce
1-2 tablespoons chopped fresh parsley or chives,
or a mixture of both
salt and freshly ground black pepper

Cook the potatoes in a saucepan of lightly salted boiling water until just tender. Drain. When cool enough to handle, remove the skins if necessary.

Mix the tomato purée with the oil, lemon juice and garlic in a bowl. Add salt, pepper and Tabasco to taste, then stir in the herbs.

Pour the dressing over the potatoes, mix lightly and leave to marinate for 3-4 hours before serving.

POTATO & COURGETTE SALAD

Serves 4

500 g (*1 lb*) new potatoes, scrubbed
250 g (*8 oz*) courgettes, sliced
4 tablespoons sunflower oil
finely grated rind and juice of 1 small orange
1 tablespoon wine vinegar
1 tablespoon chopped fresh parsley
1 tablespoon snipped fresh chives
or finely chopped spring onions
salt and freshly ground black pepper
chopped fresh parsley or snipped fresh chives,
to garnish

Cook the potatoes in a saucepan of lightly salted boiling water until tender. Using a slotted spoon, remove from the water and drain. Add the courgettes to the boiling water, simmer for 5 minutes until tender, then drain.

Put the oil in a bowl with the orange rind and juice, vinegar, parsley and chives or spring onions. Season to taste and beat well.

Cut the larger potatoes into halves; leave the small ones whole. Combine the potatoes and courgettes in a bowl, pour on the dressing and toss lightly to mix. The potatoes will absorb the flavour better if they are still warm.

Sprinkle parsley or chives over the salad just before serving. Serve cold.

POTATO SALAD AU VERMOUTH

Serves 6

1 kg (*2 lb*) small new potatoes, scrubbed
150 ml (*¼ pint*) chicken stock
4 tablespoons dry white vermouth
6 tablespoons thick mayonnaise
3 tablespoons snipped fresh chives,
chopped shallots or spring onions
2 tablespoons finely chopped fresh parsley
salt and freshly ground black pepper

Boil or steam the potatoes until tender. Mix the chicken stock and vermouth in a jug.

Peel the hot potatoes and slice them thickly. Put them into a bowl, moistening each layer with stock and vermouth. Set aside until the potatoes are quite cold and have absorbed most of the dressing.

Carefully drain off the excess liquid if any – it may be used to fortify a soup. Fold the mayonnaise and herbs carefully into the salad, to avoid breaking the potato slices, and season to taste with salt and pepper. Chill until ready to serve.

HOT POTATOES WITH BACON

Serves 6

1 kg (*2 lb*) small new potatoes, scrubbed
4 rashers rindless streaky bacon
2 tablespoons sesame seeds
2 tablespoons chopped fresh parsley
3 spring onions, sliced

DRESSING:

2 tablespoons vinegar
1 teaspoon wholegrain mustard
125 ml (*4 fl oz*) sunflower oil
salt and freshly ground black pepper

Cook the new potatoes in a saucepan of lightly salted boiling water until tender. Meanwhile, grill the bacon until crisp. Drain the bacon on kitchen paper and crumble or cut into small pieces.

Spread the sesame seeds on a piece of foil and grill until pale golden. Set aside.

To make the dressing, whisk the vinegar, salt, pepper and mustard together in a salad bowl, then gradually whisk in the oil. Drain the potatoes thoroughly and add to the dressing with the sesame seeds and parsley. Add salt and pepper to taste. Toss together gently. Scatter the bacon and spring onions over the salad and serve while still warm.

Illustrated on jacket

POTATO & BROAD BEAN SALAD

Serves 6-8

750 g (*1½ lb*) new potatoes, scrubbed
375 g (*12 oz*) frozen broad beans
75 ml (*3 fl oz*) French dressing
150 ml (*¼ pint*) thick mayonnaise
75 g (*3 oz*) pepperoni, sliced
1 bunch spring onions, finely sliced
125 g (*4 oz*) black olives
or drained pickled walnuts, quartered
salt and freshly ground black pepper

Cook the potatoes in a saucepan of salted boiling water for about 10-15 minutes until they are just tender. Drain well. Cook the broad beans in a saucepan of lightly salted boiling water until just tender. Drain.

Cut the warm potatoes into quarters and place in a bowl. Combine the dressing and the mayonnaise in a jug and season well. Pour over the potatoes and toss until coated.

Add the beans, pepperoni, spring onions and olives or pickled walnuts; toss again. Spoon the salad into a bowl. Cover and chill in the refrigerator until required.

Illustrated opposite

DAUPHINE POTATOES

Serves 6

750 g (*1½ lb*) floury potatoes, peeled
1 egg yolk
pinch of ground nutmeg
sunflower oil, for deep-frying
salt and freshly ground black pepper

CHOUX PASTRY:

100 ml (*3½ fl oz*) water
50 g (*2 oz*) butter
pinch of salt
75 g (*3 oz*) plain flour
2 eggs

To make the choux pastry, heat the water, butter and salt in a saucepan. Bring to the boil, add the flour all at once and beat to a smooth paste. Cook for 1 minute. Remove from the heat and gradually beat in the eggs to make a smooth glossy paste.

Cook the potatoes in a saucepan of lightly salted boiling water until just tender. Drain well and press through a sieve to purée them. Beat in the egg yolk and nutmeg and season to taste. Mix with the choux paste and leave to cool.

Heat the oil to 180°C (*350°F*), or until a cube of bread browns in 1 minute. Drop spoonfuls of the potato mixture into the oil and fry until golden. Drain and serve at once.

SAUTEED POTATOES WITH GARLIC

Serves 4-6

750 g (*1½ lb*) potatoes, peeled
and cut into 2.5 cm (*1 inch*) cubes
3 tablespoons olive oil
3 plump garlic cloves, peeled
coarse salt
finely chopped fresh parsley, to garnish

Rinse the potato cubes in a colander and dry thoroughly with kitchen paper.

In a large, deep frying pan that will take the potatoes in a single layer, heat the olive oil. Fry the garlic cloves slowly until they are just golden. Add the potatoes and fry, tossing constantly, over moderate heat for 5 minutes, or until coloured on all sides. Sprinkle the potatoes with salt. Half-cover the pan with a lid or foil and fry the potatoes very slowly, shaking the pan and turning them occasionally, for about 15 minutes, or until they are crisp and golden on all sides and feel soft inside when pierced with a fork or skewer.

Remove potato cubes from pan with a slotted spoon. Discard garlic cloves. Drain potatoes thoroughly and serve immediately, sprinkled with more salt and garnished with parsley.

Note: It is important not to pierce the garlic cloves, and vital that they do not burn, otherwise they will impart a bitter taste.

CAPE POTATO PUDDING

Serves 4-6

1 kg (*2 lb*) old potatoes, peeled
50 g (*2 oz*) butter or margarine
3 tablespoons milk
1 teaspoon sugar
3 eggs, beaten
1 teaspoon finely grated lemon rind
salt

Cook the potatoes in a saucepan of lightly salted boiling water until tender. Drain. Melt half the butter in a large saucepan with the milk. Add the potatoes. Mash them, then beat well until smooth. Add the sugar and slowly work in the beaten eggs and lemon rind. Add salt to taste.

Use a little of the remaining butter to grease a 1.2 litre (*2 pint*) soufflé dish. Turn the mixture into the dish and dot the surface with the remaining butter.

Bake in a preheated oven, 190°C (*375°F*), Gas Mark 5, for 25-30 minutes until lightly browned. Serve the 'pudding' immediately as an accompaniment to fish with a sauce, or roast or grilled meats.

POTATO & GREEN PEPPER RATATOUILLE

Serves 4

2 tablespoons sunflower oil
250 g (*8 oz*) potatoes, sliced
1 onion, sliced
1 green pepper, cored, seeded and sliced
1 yellow pepper, cored, seeded and sliced
750 g (*1½ lb*) plum tomatoes,
skinned and chopped
1 tablespoon soy sauce
2 tablespoons tomato purée
salt and freshly ground black pepper

Heat the oil in a saucepan and sauté the potatoes, onion and peppers for 5-10 minutes.

Add the tomatoes, soy sauce, tomato purée and salt and pepper to taste. Bring to the boil, cover and simmer for 40 minutes or until the vegetables are tender. Serve hot.

Illustrated on pages 2-3

BAKED POTATOES

Serves 4

4 large baking potatoes, scrubbed and dried
coarsely ground sea salt
freshly ground black pepper

BACON & MUSHROOM FILLING:

4 rashers rindless smoked bacon
50 g (*2 oz*) butter
125 g (*4 oz*) chestnut
or button mushrooms, chopped

SHRIMP & SPRING ONION TOPPING:

250 g (*8 oz*) cooked peeled shrimps
150 ml (*¼ pint*) soured cream
150 ml (*¼ pint*) natural yogurt
a few drops of Tabasco sauce
4 spring onions, finely chopped

SALMON & SOURED CREAM TOPPING:

250 g (*8 oz*) cold poached salmon
or drained canned salmon
300 ml (*½ pint*) soured cream
1 teaspoon lemon juice
2 teaspoons chopped fresh thyme,
or ½ teaspoon dried
25 g (*1 oz*) flaked almonds, toasted, to garnish

Prick the potatoes all over with a fork and rub with salt. Wrap each potato in individual pieces of foil if liked. Bake in a preheated oven, 200°C (*400°F*), Gas Mark 6, 1-1½ hours or until tender. Alternatively, double-wrap the potatoes in heavy-duty foil and place in the hot coals of a preheated barbecue. Bake for about 45 minutes, turning frequently.

Once cooked, remove the potatoes from the foil, if used and prepare as follows. (Each filling is sufficient for four large potatoes.)

For the bacon and mushroom filling, cut a slice lengthways from the top of each baked potato and scoop out the flesh. Grill the bacon until crisp, drain on kitchen paper and crumble. Mix with the mashed potato flesh and half the butter. Melt the remaining butter in a frying pan, add the mushrooms and fry for about 3 minutes. Remove from the heat and stir the mushrooms into the bacon and potato mixture, season to taste with salt and pepper. Return the mixture to the potato skins and return the potatoes to the oven or place on the oiled grill of the barbecue. Cook for about 10 minutes until heated through.

For the shrimp and spring onion topping, cut the baked potatoes almost in half lengthways and crossways to form a criss-cross. Combine the filling ingredients, season to taste and heap on to the potatoes.

For the salmon and soured cream topping, cut a deep criss-cross as above in the baked potatoes. Flake the cooked salmon, removing any skin and bones. Mix with the remaining topping ingredients and season to taste. Pile the mixture on top of the baked potatoes and garnish with the flaked almonds.

Illustrated opposite

POTATO, LEMON & THYME CASSEROLE

Serves 4-6

750 g (*1½ lb*) potatoes, peeled
5 tablespoons olive oil
1 large onion, sliced
2 tablespoons lemon juice
1 teaspoon grated lemon rind
150 ml (*¼ pint*) chicken stock
1 tablespoon chopped fresh thyme
salt and freshly ground black pepper

Cut the potatoes into slices approximately 1 cm (*½ inch*) thick, and then halve each slice widthways. Wash the slices and pat them dry.

Heat 3 tablespoons of the olive oil in a deep frying pan; add the sliced onions and cook until they start to colour. Add the prepared potatoes and the remaining oil and continue cooking over a moderate heat, stirring, until the onions and potatoes turn lightly golden.

Add the lemon juice, lemon rind, stock and thyme, with salt and pepper to taste. Cover and cook slowly, stirring from time to time, for 25-30 minutes, by which time the water should have evaporated and the potatoes will be sitting in a richly flavoured oil. Serve hot.

PAN HAGGERTY

Serves 6

2 tablespoons olive oil
375 g (*12 oz*) onions, thinly sliced
750 g (*1½ lb*) potatoes, peeled
25 g (*1 oz*) butter
125 g (*4 oz*) Cheddar cheese, grated
salt and freshly ground black pepper

Heat the olive oil in a frying pan, add the onions and fry over a low heat until soft and transparent. Remove from the pan.

Cut the potatoes into 3 mm (*⅛ inch*) slices and pat them dry on kitchen paper.

Melt the butter in the frying pan. Arrange the potatoes, onions and cheese in layers in the pan, reserving a little cheese for the top. Begin and end with potato slices. Season each layer with salt and pepper.

Cover the pan and cook over a low heat for 30 minutes, or until the vegetables are tender. Sprinkle the remaining cheese over the top and brown under a preheated hot grill for a few minutes. Serve at once.

POTATO & HAZELNUT BAKE

Serves 4

625 g (*1¼ lb*) potatoes, peeled
1 small onion, finely chopped
2 tablespoons chopped fresh parsley
3 tablespoons chopped hazelnuts
150 ml (*¼ pint*) chicken stock
150 ml (*¼ pint*) milk
2 eggs, beaten
40 g (*1½ oz*) Gruyère cheese, grated
salt and freshly ground black pepper

Slice the potatoes very thinly with a sharp knife, a mandolin or the slicing blade of a food processor. Layer the potato slices with the onion, parsley, 2 tablespoons of the chopped hazelnuts, and salt and pepper to taste, in a greased deep ovenproof dish.

Blend the stock with the milk and eggs in a bowl. Add salt and pepper to taste. Pour the mixture over the potatoes and sprinkle with the remaining hazelnuts. Cover the dish with foil and bake in a preheated oven, 190°C (*375°F*), Gas Mark 5, for 40 minutes (hand-sliced potatoes will be slightly thicker, and will take longer to cook).

Remove the foil and sprinkle with the grated cheese. Bake for a further 15-20 minutes, until the potatoes are golden and tender.

CHEESE CROQUETTES

Serves 4

500 g (*1 lb*) mashed potato
175 g (*6 oz*) Gruyère, Stilton
or Cheddar cheese, finely diced
1 egg yolk
3 tablespoons plain flour
1 egg, beaten
150 g (*5 oz*) fresh breadcrumbs
1 tablespoon freshly grated Parmesan cheese
sunflower oil, for frying
salt and freshly ground black pepper

Mix the potato with the cheese. Beat in the egg yolk and season to taste with salt and plenty of pepper. Shape the mixture into 16 croquettes. Roll the croquettes in the flour, dip them in the beaten egg and finally coat them thoroughly in a mixture of breadcrumbs and Parmesan. Arrange in a single layer on a plate and chill until ready to use.

Heat about 1 cm (*½ inch*) of oil in a frying pan and fry the croquettes over a medium heat for about 5-10 minutes, turning constantly so they cook evenly. When the croquettes are golden brown and crisp, remove them from the pan and drain on kitchen paper.

GAME CHIPS

Serves 4

4 potatoes, peeled
sunflower oil, for deep-frying
salt

Thinly slice the potatoes crossways with a sharp knife, a mandolin or the slicing blade of a food processor. Soak the slices in iced water for 15-20 minutes to remove the excess starch and to crisp the potatoes. Drain the potato slices and dry them thoroughly on a clean cloth or kitchen paper.

Heat the oil for deep-frying to 180-190°C (*350-375°F*), or until a cube of bread browns in 30 seconds. Place a few potato slices in the frying basket and lower into the fat. Cook for 3-5 minutes until the chips are golden brown, turning if necessary. Remove the basket and drain the chips on a cloth or piece of kitchen paper. Repeat with the remaining potato slices. Serve the game chips in a bowl, sprinkled with salt.

POTATO SKINS WITH SOURED CREAM DIP

Serves 5-10

5 large baking potatoes, scrubbed and dried
150 ml (*¼ pint*) soured cream
1 teaspoon snipped fresh chives
sunflower oil, for frying
salt and freshly ground black pepper
snipped fresh chives, to garnish

Prick the potatoes with a fork. Bake on the shelves of a preheated oven, 200°C (*400°F*), Gas Mark 6, for about 1¼ hours until tender.

Meanwhile, prepare the dip. In a bowl, mix the soured cream with the chives. Season to taste. Cover the bowl and leave to chill.

When the potatoes are cooked, cool for a few minutes, cut each one into quarters lengthways. Scoop out most of the potato flesh, leaving a thin layer next to the skin. (The scooped-out potato may be used to top a pie.)

Pour the oil into a small frying pan to a depth of 7.5 cm (*3 inches*). Heat the oil to 180-190°C (*350-375°F*), or until a cube of bread browns in 30 seconds. Add the potato skins carefully to the hot oil. Fry for about 2 minutes until brown and crisp. Remove, drain on kitchen paper. To serve, arrange on a plate with the dip, sprinkled with chives, in the centre.

Illustrated opposite

LEEK, POTATO & CORIANDER BAKE

Serves 4

2 tablespoons sunflower oil
25 g (*1 oz*) butter
500 g (*1 lb*) leeks, trimmed, washed
and cut into 2 cm (*¾ inch*) rings
1 kg (*2 lb*) small waxy potatoes,
such as Cyprus or Jersey, scrubbed
and cut into 1 cm (*½ inch*) slices
1 teaspoon black peppercorns
2 teaspoons coriander seeds
1 teaspoon sea salt

Put the oil and butter in a large shallow roasting tin and place in a preheated oven, 200°C (*400°F*), Gas Mark 6, until the butter is just melted. Add the prepared leeks and potatoes, turning them over several times to coat them with the oil and butter. Level the mixture in the tin.

Crush the peppercorns with the coriander seeds. (If you have no pestle and mortar, put the seeds and peppercorns between two double sheets of kitchen paper or greaseproof paper and crush with a rolling pin.) Tip the mixture into a bowl and stir in the salt. Sprinkle the spice mixture over the vegetables and mix lightly. Cook for 45-50 minutes, or until the potatoes are nicely browned.

POTATO HERB SCONES

Makes 8

375 g (*12 oz*) potatoes, peeled
15 g (*½ oz*) butter
2 tablespoons snipped fresh chives
2 tablespoons chopped fresh parsley
75 g (*3 oz*) plain or wholemeal flour
a little milk (optional)
sunflower oil, for frying
salt and freshly ground black pepper

Cook potatoes in a saucepan of lightly salted boiling water for 15-20 minutes until tender. Drain. Put the potatoes in a bowl and mash with the butter. Add salt and pepper to taste and stir in the chives and parsley. Beat in the flour. Add a little milk if the mixture is dry.

Form the potato mixture into a ball and knead lightly until it is smooth and free from cracks. Roll out on a lightly floured board to a thickness of 5 mm (*¼ inch*). Prick the surface all over with a fork and cut into neat triangle shapes.

Lightly oil a heavy-based frying pan, heat and cook the potato triangles, a few at a time, for 3 minutes on each side until golden brown.

POTATOES BRAISED IN RED WINE

Serves 4

**750 g (*1½ lb*) potatoes, peeled and
cut into 5 mm (*¼ inch*) slices
300 ml (*½ pint*) dry red wine
2 tablespoons chopped fresh thyme
2 tablespoons chopped fresh parsley
salt and freshly ground black pepper**

Place the potato slices in a casserole or ovenproof dish and pour in the red wine. Sprinkle with the chopped fresh herbs and salt and pepper to taste. Mix lightly so that all the potatoes are coated with wine and herbs.

Cover the casserole or dish with a lid or foil. Bake in a preheated oven, 190°C (*375°F*), Gas Mark 5, for about 1 hour, or until the potatoes are tender and almost all the wine has been absorbed. Stir twice during cooking. The potatoes will be a delicate pink colour on the outside but still white inside. Serve hot.

AUBERGINE & POTATO CASSEROLE

Serves 4

**2 aubergines, thinly sliced
500 g (*1 lb*) potatoes, peeled and thinly sliced
1 small onion, grated
125 g (*4 oz*) Gruyère cheese, grated
150 ml (*¼ pint*) chicken or vegetable stock
1 tablespoon sunflower oil
salt and freshly ground black pepper**

Spread out the aubergine slices in a colander and sprinkle them liberally with salt. Leave for at least 30 minutes, then wash the slices and drain well.

In an ovenproof casserole arrange layers of the potato and aubergine slices, sprinkling each layer with a little of the grated onion, Gruyère and salt and pepper. Arrange the top layer so that there are alternate slices of potato and aubergine overlapping in a circle.

Pour in the chicken or vegetable stock and brush the top layer with the oil. Cover the casserole dish with foil and bake in a preheated oven, 190°C (*375°F*), Gas Mark 5, for 30 minutes. Remove the foil and cook for 30-45 minutes, or until the vegetables are tender and the top is brown.

POTATOES DAUPHINOISE

Serves 4-6

**750 g-1 kg (*1½-2 lb*) evenly shaped potatoes,
peeled and thinly sliced
1 garlic clove, peeled and halved
butter, for greasing
1 teaspoon freshly grated nutmeg
300 ml (*½ pint*) single cream
75 g (*3 oz*) Gruyère cheese, grated
salt and freshly ground black pepper**

Cook the potatoes in a saucepan of lightly salted boiling water for 5 minutes. Drain and cool slightly.

Rub the cut garlic clove around the inside of a deep ovenproof dish. Grease the dish with plenty of butter. Arrange the potatoes in layers, sprinkling each layer with nutmeg and salt and pepper.

Pour the cream over the potatoes. Sprinkle the cheese over the surface so that the potatoes are completely covered. Cook, covered, in the centre of a preheated oven, 180°C (*350°F*), Gas Mark 4, for about 1-1¼ hours, or until the potatoes are cooked through and the cheese topping is crusty and golden brown, uncovering the dish after 45 minutes.

Illustrated on pages 2-3

FANTAIL POTATOES

Serves 4-8

**8 baking potatoes,
about 175-250 g (*6-8 oz*) each,
peeled and halved lengthways
4 tablespoons olive oil
8 garlic cloves, unpeeled
10-12 thyme sprigs
salt**

Place the potatoes cut-side down. Using a sharp knife make cuts at 5 mm (*¼ inch*) intervals along the length of each potato almost through to the base, just leaving a hinge to hold them together.

Heat the oil in a roasting tin in a preheated oven, 200°C (*400°F*), Gas Mark 6, until hot. Add the potatoes to the tin and spoon the oil evenly over each one. Roast the potatoes for 30 minutes. Baste well and sprinkle with a little salt, if liked.

Add the garlic and thyme and cook for a further 30 minutes or so until the potatoes are golden brown and crisp; the cuts will open out a little to create the fantail shape from which the recipe takes its name.

Illustrated opposite

ROSTI

Serves 4

1 kg (*2 lb*) even-sized floury potatoes, scrubbed
75 g (*3 oz*) butter
1 small mild onion, very finely chopped
salt and freshly ground black pepper

Cook the potatoes in a saucepan of lightly salted boiling water for 7 minutes. Drain. When the potatoes are quite cold, peel them and grate coarsely into a bowl.

Heat 15 g (*½ oz*) of the butter in a large, heavy-based frying pan. Add the onion and cook for about 5 minutes until soft. Stir into the potato and season.

Melt the remaining butter in the frying pan. Set aside about 1 tablespoon of the melted butter in a cup. Add the potato mixture and form into a neat cake. Fry gently, shaking the pan occasionally so that the rösti cake does not stick, for about 15 minutes longer, or until the underside of the cake is a crusty golden brown. To cook the top, pour over the reserved melted butter and either place under a preheated grill to brown, or turn in the pan and brown. To serve, invert the rösti cake on to a flat heated dish and cut it into wedges.

Illustrated on page 1

HERB-BAKED NEW POTATOES

Serves 4

750 g (*1½ lb*) new potatoes, scrubbed
sea salt
freshly ground black pepper
4 mint sprigs
4 parsley sprigs
TO GARNISH:
1 tablespoon chopped fresh mint
1 tablespoon chopped fresh parsley

Grease a sheet of foil large enough to enclose the potatoes. Put the potatoes into the centre and sprinkle them with the sea salt and pepper. Put the mint and parsley sprigs among the potatoes. Fold the foil around the potatoes and seal the edges.

Bake the potatoes in a preheated oven, 200°C (*400°F*), Gas Mark 6, for 40-45 minutes, until they are tender.

Remove the potatoes from the foil and place them in a serving dish. Sprinkle with the chopped mint and parsley and serve.

SOUFFLE CHEESE POTATOES

Serves 4

4 baking potatoes, scrubbed and dried
20 g (¾ oz) butter
125 g (4 oz) curd cheese
2 tablespoons freshly grated Parmesan cheese
2 teaspoons French or wholegrain mustard
2 eggs, separated
salt and freshly ground black pepper

Prick the potatoes with a fork. Place on a baking sheet and bake in a preheated oven, 190°C (*375°F*), Gas Mark 5, for about 1¼ hours, until tender.

Cut a lengthways slice from the top of each potato; carefully scoop most of the potato flesh into a bowl, leaving a shell.

Mash the potato flesh with the butter. Add the curd cheese, 1 tablespoon of Parmesan, the mustard and the egg yolks. Stir in salt and pepper to taste.

Whisk the egg whites in a grease-free bowl until stiff but not dry; fold lightly into the potato mixture. Spoon into the potato shells, then sprinkle with the remaining Parmesan.

Return the potatoes to the oven for a further 15-20 minutes, until well risen, golden and puffed. Serve immediately.

NEW POTATOES WITH FENNEL & MINT

Serves 6

1 kg (2 lb) tiny new potatoes,
preferably Jersey or English, scrubbed
15 g (½ oz) butter
1 small fennel bulb, trimmed and finely chopped
2 tablespoons chopped fresh mint
salt and freshly ground black pepper
mint sprigs, to garnish

Cook the potatoes in a saucepan of lightly salted boiling water until just tender. Drain.

Put the butter into the warm pan and heat gently. Add the fennel and fry for about 5 minutes until just beginning to brown. Season well with pepper.

Tip the cooked potatoes into the pan, add the chopped mint and toss the potatoes so that they are coated with butter, mint and fennel. Serve hot, garnished with sprigs of mint.

NEW POTATO CURRY

Serves 4

5 cm (*2 inch*) piece of fresh root ginger
2 garlic cloves, crushed
50 g (*2 oz*) ghee or butter
2 large onions, finely chopped
2 bay leaves
1 stick cinnamon,
broken into short lengths
2 teaspoons fennel seeds
3 green cardamoms
1 teaspoon turmeric
1 kg (*2 lb*) small new potatoes, scrubbed
600 ml (*1 pint*) water
300 ml (*½ pint*) natural yogurt
salt and freshly ground black pepper

TO GARNISH:

chilli powder
chopped fresh coriander leaves

Mix the grated ginger and crushed garlic together in a small bowl.

Place the ghee or butter in a large saucepan or wok and heat. Add the chopped onions, the ginger mixture, bay leaves, broken cinnamon stick, fennel seeds, cardamoms and turmeric to the melted fat. Fry the mixture gently, stirring constantly, until the onion is soft but not browned.

Add the scrubbed potatoes to the saucepan or wok, pour in the measured water and season with salt and pepper to taste. Bring the mixture to the boil and cover.

Simmer the curry steadily for 10 minutes, then uncover the pan and cook fairly rapidly for a further 10 minutes, or until most of the water has evaporated.

Pour the natural yogurt over the potatoes and heat through fairly gently, to avoid curdling the sauce.

Transfer the curry to a serving dish and sprinkle with chilli powder to taste and chopped fresh coriander before serving.

Illustrated opposite

POTATO & CAULIFLOWER CURRY

Serves 6-8

**500 g (*1 lb*) potatoes, peeled and
cut into 2.5 cm (*1 inch*) pieces
500 g (*1 lb*) cauliflower, separated into
small florets, thick stalk discarded
75 g (*3 oz*) ghee or butter
1 onion, finely chopped
2 garlic cloves, finely chopped
5 cm (*2 inch*) piece of fresh root ginger,
peeled and finely chopped
2 teaspoons ground coriander
1 teaspoon kalonji (onion seeds) (optional)
1 teaspoon turmeric
1 teaspoon chilli powder
3 tablespoons tomato purée
2 teaspoons garam masala
salt and freshly ground black pepper**

Cook the potato chunks and cauliflower florets in separate saucepans of lightly salted boiling water until the vegetables just begin to soften. Drain the potato and cauliflower, reserving the cauliflower water.

Meanwhile, heat the ghee or butter in a heavy-based saucepan. Add the chopped onion and garlic to the pan and cook for 3 minutes. Stir in the finely chopped ginger and fry gently for 2-3 minutes. Add the ground coriander and kalonji, if using, and fry for a further 30 seconds. Add the turmeric, chilli powder and 1 teaspoon each of freshly ground black pepper and salt. Stir well and fry for a further 2 minutes. Stir the tomato purée into the mixture.

Add the cooked potato and cauliflower to the saucepan with 150 ml (*5 fl oz*) of the cauliflower water and toss gently in the spice mixture. If the curry becomes too dry, add a little more of the reserved cauliflower water.

Cook for 5-6 minutes, then sprinkle in the garam masala and cook for a further minute. Serve the curry hot with boiled rice and a selection of accompaniments.

AUBERGINE & POTATO CURRY

Serves 4

350 g (*12 oz*) aubergine, cubed
2 teaspoons salt
3 tablespoons sunflower oil
½-1 teaspoon chilli powder
1 teaspoon turmeric
2 teaspoons ground cumin
2 teaspoons ground coriander
2.5 cm (*1 inch*) piece of fresh root ginger,
peeled and finely chopped
375 g (*12 oz*) potatoes, peeled and cubed
250 g (*8 oz*) can tomatoes
2 tablespoons lemon juice
2 tablespoons chopped fresh coriander leaves
1 teaspoon garam masala

Place the aubergine in a colander, sprinkle with 1 teaspoon of the salt and set aside for 20 minutes. Rinse under cold water and drain.

Heat the oil in a saucepan, add the chilli powder, turmeric, ground cumin, coriander and ginger and fry over a gentle heat for 2 minutes. Add the potatoes and drained aubergine and fry, stirring, for 2 minutes.

Add the canned tomatoes, lemon juice, chopped fresh coriander and remaining salt. Cover and simmer for 25 minutes or until the vegetables are tender. Just before serving, stir in the garam masala.

POTATO SALLIS

Serves 5-6 as a snack

750 g (*1½ lb*) potatoes
sunflower oil, for deep-frying
2 tablespoons garam masala
2 teaspoons sea salt
½-2 teaspoons chilli powder (optional)

Slice two potatoes at a time into very thin matchsticks, using a chip-cutter or a knife – do not prepare more than two at a time, or they will discolour.

Heat the oil for deep-frying to 180-190°C (*350-375°F*), or until a cube of bread browns in 30 seconds. Immediately add the potato chips and fry for 3-5 minutes, or until golden.

Lift the sallis out of the oil, drain and place on kitchen paper to remove excess oil. Repeat the process until all the potatoes have been used. Sprinkle with garam masala, sea salt and chilli powder to taste, if using. Serve the sallis immediately, while hot.

POTATO SAMOSAS

Makes 40

PASTRY:

500 g (*1 lb*) plain flour
½ teaspoon baking powder
1 teaspoon salt
25 g (*1 oz*) butter, melted
4 tablespoons natural yogurt
about 8 tablespoons tepid water

FILLING:

50 g (*2 oz*) butter
2 small onions, finely chopped
750 g (*1½ lb*) cooked potatoes,
peeled and finely diced
½-1 fresh green chilli, seeded
and finely chopped
2 teaspoons garam masala
3 teaspoons desiccated coconut
sunflower oil, for deep-frying
salt and freshly ground black pepper

Sift the flour with the baking powder and salt into a mixing bowl. Make a well in the centre and add the melted butter and yogurt. Draw the flour into the liquid, using a wooden spoon, adding water as necessary to make a smooth dough. Knead until free from cracks and set aside.

To make the filling, melt the butter in a large frying pan, add the onion and cook over a gentle heat for 5 minutes until soft and lightly coloured, then add the potatoes and chillies and fry until golden brown, turning frequently. Add the garam masala and coconut, and season with salt. Stir well to mix and leave to cool.

On a lightly floured board or work surface roll 20 balls of dough the size of a shelled walnut into thin circles, 15 cm (*6 inches*) in diameter. Cut each circle in half. Shape each semi-circle into a cone and fill with a little of the potato mixture. Dampen the top edges with water and press together firmly to seal.

Heat the oil for deep-frying to 180-190°C (*350-375°F*), or until a cube of bread browns in 30 seconds. Deep-fry the samosas, a few at a time, until golden brown all over. Drain on kitchen paper and serve hot, sprinkled with freshly ground black pepper.

Illustrated opposite

POTATO PANCAKES

Serves 4-6

500 g (*1 lb*) potatoes, peeled
4 tablespoons boiling milk
50 g (*2 oz*) plain flour
4 eggs, beaten
½ teaspoon dried mixed herbs
4 tablespoons double cream
sunflower oil, for frying
salt and freshly ground black pepper
parsley sprig, to garnish

Cook the potatoes in a saucepan of lightly salted boiling water until tender. Drain well, then mash until very smooth. Beat in the boiling milk and leave to cool completely.

Using a wooden spoon, beat in the flour and eggs. Stir in the herbs and cream, and season with salt and pepper. Beat until very smooth – the mixture should resemble a thick batter.

Heat the oil in a large frying pan and swirl it around. When the oil begins to give off a slight haze, drop in tablespoons of the batter, a little apart, and cook for 2 minutes on each side, until golden brown.

Place the pancakes in layers in a clean dry tea towel and keep warm in a preheated oven, 140°C (*275°F*), Gas Mark 1. Repeat with the remaining batter. Serve the pancakes very hot, garnished with parsley.

SPANISH OMELETTE

Serves 4-6

125 ml (*4 fl oz*) olive oil
500 g (*1 lb*) potatoes, peeled and
chopped or sliced
2 onions, chopped
1 red pepper, cored, seeded and chopped
or cut into strips
1 green pepper, cored, seeded and chopped
or cut into strips
2-3 garlic cloves, crushed or finely chopped
375 g (*12 oz*) tomatoes,
skinned and finely chopped
6 eggs
salt

Heat 5 tablespoons of the oil in a large saucepan, add the potatoes and fry over a low heat, turning frequently, for about 15 minutes.

Meanwhile, heat the remaining oil in a large non-stick frying pan. Add the onions and peppers, and fry over a low heat for about 8-10 minutes. Just before the vegetables are cooked, add the garlic, tomatoes and cooked potatoes. Mix lightly.

Beat the eggs in a bowl with a little salt. Pour the mixture evenly over the vegetables and cook, over a low heat, until the egg has just set. Turn the omelette out on to a large plate and serve, cut into wedges.

PUMPKIN & POTATO PIE

Serves 6-8

**500 g (*1 lb*) pumpkin, peeled,
seeded and cubed
50 g (*2 oz*) butter
1 large onion, sliced
375 g (*12 oz*) potatoes, scrubbed
500 g (*1 lb*) packet frozen puff pastry, thawed
1 egg, beaten
salt and freshly ground black pepper**

Place the pumpkin cubes in a saucepan with water to cover. Add a large pinch of salt. Bring to the boil, then lower the heat and cook gently until soft – about 15 minutes. Drain very thoroughly then return the cubes to the saucepan.

Meanwhile, melt the butter in a frying pan, add the sliced onion and cook gently until soft and golden brown. Add to the pumpkin, stirring well to mix.

Cook the potatoes in a saucepan of lightly salted boiling water until almost tender. Drain and allow to cool slightly. Peel the potatoes and cut them into 1 cm (*½ inch*) dice. Stir the diced potato into the pumpkin mixture, with salt and pepper to taste.

Roll the pastry out thinly and cut out two circles – one measuring 25 cm (*10 inches*) in diameter, the other 30 cm (*12 inches*) in diameter. Place the smaller circle on a greased baking sheet. Spread the pumpkin filling over the pastry, leaving a 1 cm (*½ inch*) border of pastry round the outside of the circle and piling the filling in the centre.

Brush the pastry border with beaten egg, then place the second circle of pastry on top. Press well to seal and scallop the edges with a knife. Any remaining pastry scraps can be cut into shapes to decorate the top.

Chill the pie for 15 minutes, then brush it with the rest of the beaten egg. Place the pie in a preheated oven, 220°C (*425°F*), Gas Mark 7, and bake for 15 minutes, then reduce the heat to 190°C (*375°F*), Gas Mark 5, and bake for a further 15 minutes, until the pastry is crisp and brown.

Transfer the pie to a serving plate, cut into wedges and serve hot.

GNOCCHI DI PATATE

Serves 3-4

750 g (*1½ lb*) floury potatoes, peeled
25 g (*1 oz*) butter
1 egg, lightly beaten
½ teaspoon baking powder
175 g (*6 oz*) plain flour
8 tablespoons melted butter
6 tablespoons freshly grated Parmesan cheese
2 tablespoons fine dry breadcrumbs
salt and freshly ground black pepper
salad leaves, to garnish

TOMATO SAUCE:

425 g (*14 oz*) can chopped tomatoes
3 tablespoons tomato purée
½ teaspoon dried oregano

Cook potatoes in lightly salted boiling water until just tender. Drain well and mash to a purée with the butter. Beat in the egg and baking powder, season generously with salt.

Start adding the flour to the potato purée, a handful at a time, working it in smoothly with your fingers. As the purée stiffens, turn it out on to a board dusted with more of the flour. Continue kneading in as much of the remaining flour as is needed to make a manageable dough – it may not be necessary to use it all. Divide the dough into four portions and let them 'rest' for 10 minutes.

Meanwhile, put a large saucepan of lightly salted water on to boil. Have a kettle of water simmering in readiness and the grill hot, with four individual baking dishes warming beneath it.

To make the gnocchi, shape a portion of the dough into a cylinder measuring roughly 1-1.5 cm (*½-¾ inches*) in diameter. Cut it into 2.5 cm (*1 inch*) lengths. Alternatively, shape the dough into a solid triangular 'roll', about 3.5 cm (*1½ inches*) along each side. Cut this into 1 cm (*½ inch*) wide slices. Repeat with the remaining dough.

Place the tomato sauce ingredients in a small saucepan and heat gently. Bring to the boil and simmer for 5 minutes. Season to taste.

Drop the gnocchi into the saucepan of boiling water. They will first sink to the bottom and then float to the surface. Once they have done so, simmer them for 3 minutes. With a slotted spoon, transfer the gnocchi to a colander. Rinse them with boiling water and drain well.

Pour 1 tablespoon of the melted butter into each hot baking dish. Using all of the gnocchi and tomato sauce, layer the gnocchi and sauce in each dish. Sprinkle with the remaining butter, the Parmesan and the breadcrumbs. Place the dishes back under the grill to brown and crisp the tops. Sprinkle with black pepper and serve hot with a salad garnish.

Illustrated opposite

POTATO &
SAUSAGEMEAT
BRAID

Serves 4-6

PASTRY:

175 g (*6 oz*) plain flour

½ teaspoon salt

75 g (*3 oz*) margarine

75 g (*3 oz*) mashed potato, sieved

beaten egg, to glaze

FILLING:

500 g (*1 lb*) pork sausagemeat

4 tablespoons chutney or pickle

250 g (*8 oz*) cooked potatoes, sliced

50 g (*2 oz*) Cheddar cheese, grated

salt and freshly ground black pepper

To make the potato pastry, sift the flour and salt together into a large mixing bowl. Gently rub in the margarine with your fingertips until the mixture resembles fine breadcrumbs. Then work in the sieved mashed potato to make a firm dough.

Place the pastry on a lightly floured surface, and roll out to a 30 cm (*12 inch*) square. Carefully place the pastry on a baking sheet and mark into three pieces lengthways.

Season the pork sausagemeat with salt and pepper and spread it down the centre section of the pastry. Cover the sausagemeat with the chutney or pickle then lay the slices of cooked potato and grated cheese on top.

Make a series of diagonal cuts in the pastry 2.5 cm (*1 inch*) apart on either side of the sausagemeat, to within 1 cm (*½ inch*) of the filling. Brush the strips with water and bring them to the middle, plaiting them over the sausagemeat filling. Press the ends together to seal and trim.

Brush the braid with the beaten egg and bake in a preheated oven, 220°C (*425°F*), Gas Mark 7, for 15 minutes, then reduce the heat to 200°C (*400°F*), Gas Mark 6, and bake for a further 25-30 minutes. Serve hot with a selection of vegetables, or cold with a salad.

ALMOND POTATOES

Serves 4

**375 g (*12 oz*) potatoes, cooked
and mashed with milk and butter
seasoned flour, for coating
1 egg, beaten
125 g (*4 oz*) almonds, finely chopped
25 g (*1 oz*) butter
1 tablespoon sunflower oil
salt and freshly ground black pepper
parsley sprigs, to garnish**

Divide the mashed potato into 12 pieces. Place the flour on a plate. Shape each potato piece into a medallion shape, coating it with flour as you do so. Dip each medallion in the beaten egg and then the almonds.

Heat the butter and oil in a large frying pan and cook the medallions, a few at a time, for about 6 minutes, turning once, until golden. Drain on kitchen paper. Serve hot, garnished with sprigs of parsley.

STIR-FRIED POTATOES

Serves 4

**500 g (*1 lb*) potatoes, grated
and rinsed to extract the starch
3 tablespoons sunflower oil
375 g (*12 oz*) vegetables, such as onion,
cauliflower, peppers, runner beans, sweetcorn,
broccoli, celery, courgettes, parsnip,
mushrooms, cabbage or leeks, finely chopped
2 tablespoons soy sauce
2.5 cm (*1 inch*) piece of fresh root
ginger, grated
salt and freshly ground black pepper**

Use a cloth to squeeze the excess moisture from the grated potato. Heat the oil in a large non-stick pan or wok. Fry the grated potato for 5-10 minutes or until nearly cooked, stirring frequently.

Add the chosen vegetables, soy sauce, ginger and salt and pepper and fry briskly for a further 5-10 minutes to cook the vegetables yet still keeping them crisp. Serve hot.

LANCASHIRE HOTPOT

Serves 6

3 tablespoons sunflower oil
1 kg (*2 lb*) middle neck of lamb cutlets,
trimmed of excess fat, and
tossed in 3 tablespoons seasoned flour
2 lambs' kidneys, cored and sliced
4 onions, finely sliced
250 g (*8 oz*) carrots, diced
750 g (*1½ lb*) potatoes, scrubbed and sliced
1 bay leaf
½ teaspoon dried marjoram
½ teaspoon dried thyme
450 ml (*¾ pint*) light stock
salt and freshly ground black pepper

Heat 2 tablespoons oil in a frying pan and brown the flour-coated cutlets, a few at a time. Lightly brown the kidneys. Layer the lamb, onions, kidneys, carrots and potatoes in a large casserole, seasoning each layer lightly with herbs, salt and pepper. Finish with a layer of potato slices.

Heat the stock in the frying pan then pour into the casserole. Brush the potatoes with the remaining oil. Cover the dish and cook in a preheated oven, 160°C (*325°F*), Gas Mark 3, for 2 hours, until the meat is tender. Remove the lid, increase the heat to 200°C (*400°F*), Gas Mark 6, and cook for a further 30 minutes to brown the potatoes.

PORK BAKE

Serves 4-6

4 rashers rindless streaky bacon, chopped
1 large onion, chopped
125 g (*4 oz*) mushrooms, quartered
1 teaspoon chopped fresh sage,
or ½ teaspoon dried
1 teaspoon chopped fresh thyme,
or ½ teaspoon dried
500 g (*1 lb*) lean pork, cubed and
tossed in 2 tablespoons seasoned flour
500 g (*1 lb*) potatoes, peeled and sliced
300 ml (*½ pint*) chicken stock
25 g (*1 oz*) butter, cut into small pieces
salt and freshly ground black pepper

Fry bacon in a frying pan for 3 minutes. Add the onion, cook until soft. Add mushrooms, herbs and seasoning, cook 1 minute. Remove mixture using a slotted spoon, set aside. Add pork to pan and brown. Add bacon mixture.

Put one-third of mixture into the bottom of a casserole. Cover with a layer of potatoes. Repeat layering twice more. Pour over the stock. Dot top layer of potatoes with butter.

Cover the casserole. Bake in a preheated oven, 180°C (*350°F*), Gas Mark 4, for 1½ hours, then remove the lid and bake for 15 minutes more, to brown the potato topping.

Illustrated opposite

STOVED CHICKEN

Serves 4-6

75 g (*3 oz*) butter
8 boneless chicken breast fillets, halved and
tossed in 50 g (*2 oz*) seasoned flour
1 kg (*2 lb*) potatoes, peeled and thinly sliced
1 large onion, thinly sliced
600 ml (*1 pint*) chicken stock
salt and freshly ground black pepper

Melt half of the butter in a flameproof casserole. Add the flour-coated chicken pieces and brown for 10 minutes, turning. Transfer the pieces to a plate. Remove the casserole from the heat.

Arrange one-third of the potato slices in the casserole. Melt the remaining butter and brush one-third over the potatoes, season. Arrange half the onion slices on the potatoes. Place eight of the chicken pieces on the onions. Arrange half the remaining potato slices over the chicken pieces. Brush with half the remaining melted butter, then season. Repeat the onion, chicken and potato layers. Brush with the remaining butter, then season.

Pour the stock over to just cover the potatoes. Cover with greased greaseproof paper and the casserole lid. Cook in a preheated oven, 150°C (*300°F*), Gas Mark 2, for 2 hours. Uncover the casserole, increase heat to 190°C (*375°F*), Gas Mark 5, and cook for 30 minutes more.

CORSICAN CHICKEN

Serves 6

175 g (*6 oz*) rindless back bacon,
cut into large dice
1.5 kg (*3 lb*) chicken
25 g (*1 oz*) butter
250 g (*8 oz*) button mushrooms
3 garlic cloves, crushed
1 teaspoon chopped fresh basil,
or ½ teaspoon dried
425 g (*14 oz*) can chopped tomatoes
175 ml (*6 fl oz*) chicken stock
50 g (*2 oz*) black olives, pitted
500 g (*1 lb*) small new potatoes, scraped
2 tablespoons brandy
salt and freshly ground black pepper

Heat the bacon in a flameproof casserole over a gentle heat until the fat runs. Raise the heat, fry the bacon until crisp, then remove. Add the chicken and butter to the casserole. Brown the chicken on all sides. Add the mushrooms, garlic and basil, season to taste. Cover the casserole and cook in a preheated oven, 190°C (*375°F*), Gas Mark 5, for 30 minutes.

Add the canned tomatoes, bacon, stock, olives, potatoes and brandy. Stir well, cover and cook for a further 30 minutes. Remove the lid and cook for 30 minutes more. Remove the chicken from the casserole and carve into six pieces. Spoon the sauce over the chicken and serve.

CHICKEN & HOT PEPPER POTATO GOUGERE

Serves 4

500 g (*1 lb*) potatoes, peeled
15 g (*½ oz*) butter
4 tablespoons water
40 g (*1½ oz*) plain flour
1 egg, beaten
50 g (*2 oz*) Stilton, Gorgonzola
or other blue cheese, crumbled

FILLING:

25 g (*1 oz*) butter
1 small onion, finely chopped
1 red pepper, cored, seeded and diced,
or ½ x 325 g (*11 oz*) jar whole sweet red
peppers in brine, drained and diced
20 g (*¾ oz*) plain flour
150 ml (*¼ pint*) chicken stock
150 ml (*¼ pint*) milk
500 g (*1 lb*) cooked chicken,
cut into bite-sized pieces
salt and freshly ground black pepper

Cook the potatoes in a saucepan of lightly salted boiling water until tender. Drain very thoroughly, then return to the empty pan and dry over a low heat for 1-2 minutes. Press the potatoes through a sieve into a bowl or mash them thoroughly.

Put the butter into a small pan with the water and a generous pinch of salt. Heat until the butter has melted, then bring to the boil. Quickly tip in the flour all at once and beat well until the mixture leaves the sides of the pan. Gradually beat in the egg, then beat this mixture into the mashed potato, add the blue cheese and mix well. Thoroughly grease a large oval baking dish and place spoonfuls of the mixture around the outer edge of the dish.

To make the filling, melt the butter in a saucepan, add the chopped onion and fresh pepper, if using, and fry over a gentle heat for 4-5 minutes until soft. Stir in the flour and cook for 1 minute. Gradually add the stock and milk, stirring until the mixture boils and thickens. Lower the heat and simmer for 3-4 minutes. Season, then stir in the chicken and drained peppers in brine, if using.

Spoon the filling into the centre of the gougère. Bake in a preheated oven, 220°C (*425°F*), Gas Mark 7, for 20-25 minutes until crisp and golden.

SUMMERTIME
PRAWN POTATOES

Serves 4

1 kg (*2 lb*) small new potatoes, scrubbed
600 ml (*1 pint*) chicken stock
375 g (*12 oz*) cooked ham, diced
500 g (*1 lb*) cooked peeled prawns
1 tablespoon white wine vinegar
2 teaspoons chopped fresh mint
2 tablespoons chopped fresh parsley
4 spring onions, finely chopped
salt and freshly ground black pepper

Cook the potatoes in the boiling stock in a saucepan until just tender. Meanwhile, mix the ham with the prawns in a bowl. As soon as the potatoes are cooked, remove them from the pan, using a slotted spoon, and set aside.

Bring the stock to the boil in the open pan and boil rapidly until it is reduced by half. Add the vinegar, ham and prawns. Return the potatoes to the pan and heat through gently for 1 minute, then add the herbs and spring onions. Stir well to combine all the ingredients, taste and adjust the seasoning if necessary, adding salt and pepper to taste. Serve immediately with brown bread and a green salad.

BAKED RED
SNAPPER WITH
POTATOES & OLIVES

Serves 4

500 g (*1 lb*) potatoes, peeled
and very thinly sliced
2 lemons, sliced
75 g (*3 oz*) butter
1 large or 4 small red snapper, cleaned
175 g (*6 oz*) pitted black and green olives
olive oil, for sprinkling
salt and freshly ground black pepper
dill sprigs, to garnish

Arrange the sliced potatoes and lemons in a layer in the bottom of a large greased shallow baking dish or roasting tin and dot generously with butter.

Place the fish on top of the potatoes. Season with salt and pepper and scatter the olives over the snapper. Sprinkle the fish generously with olive oil and bake in a preheated oven, 190°C (*375°F*), Gas Mark 5, for 30-40 minutes depending on the size of the fish, or until the flesh flakes easily and is tender. Serve at once, sprinkled with dill.

Illustrated opposite

PAN-FRIED BUBBLY WITH SARDINES

Serves 4

750 g (*1½ lb*) potatoes,
cooked and mashed
1 egg, beaten
1 small onion, grated
3 tablespoons sunflower oil
1 large green pepper
250 g (*8 oz*) can tomatoes
1 tablespoon tomato purée
½ teaspoon dried mixed herbs
8 fresh sardines, cleaned
50 g (*2 oz*) Cheddar cheese, grated
salt and freshly ground black pepper
1 tablespoon chopped fresh parsley, to garnish

Combine the mashed potato, beaten egg and grated onion together in a large bowl. Add salt and pepper to taste.

Heat the oil in a large frying pan with a flameproof handle, add the potato mixture and smooth with a knife or spatula. Gently fry in the oil for 10-15 minutes until golden brown underneath.

Meanwhile, scorch the skin of the green pepper under a hot grill. Transfer the pepper to a bowl and cover with several layers of kitchen paper. When cold, peel the skin off the pepper, then cut the pepper lengthways into strips. Set aside.

Mix the canned tomatoes, tomato purée and dried mixed herbs together in a small saucepan and heat gently. Pour the tomato mixture over the potatoes in the frying pan. On top of this form a wheel shape with the sardines, with their heads pointing outwards, and arrange strips of green pepper between each sardine.

Position the frying pan under a preheated grill, and grill the bubbly under a moderate heat for 6-8 minutes, or until the sardines are cooked. Sprinkle the grated Cheddar cheese over the top, increase the heat and grill until the top is golden and bubbling.

Garnish the bubbly with the chopped parsley and cut into wedges. Serve at once.

JANSSON'S TEMPTATION

Serves 4-6

8 potatoes, cut into 5 mm (*¼ inch*) thick strips
2 onions, finely chopped
2 x 50 g (*2 oz*) cans anchovy fillets
200 ml (*7 fl oz*) whipping or single cream
25 g (*1 oz*) butter
50 g (*2 oz*) fresh breadcrumbs
freshly ground black pepper

Arrange the potatoes, onions and anchovy fillets in a greased ovenproof dish, with a layer of potatoes as the topping. Season the cream with pepper. Pour over the potatoes. Melt the butter, mix with the breadcrumbs and sprinkle over the top of the potatoes.

Bake in the centre of a preheated oven, 180-190°C (*350-375°F*), Gas Mark 4-5, for 1¼ hours until the potatoes are soft.

CRAB CAKES

Serves 4

1 onion, finely chopped
50 g (*2 oz*) mushrooms, chopped
50 g (*2 oz*) butter or margarine
50 g (*2 oz*) plain flour
150 ml (*¼ pint*) milk
1 teaspoon Worcestershire sauce
2 tablespoons chopped parsley
250 g (*8 oz*) fresh, canned or frozen crabmeat
250 g (*8 oz*) cooked old potatoes,
mashed without any additional liquid
2 eggs, beaten
75 g (*3 oz*) dry natural breadcrumbs
4 tablespoons sunflower oil, or 50 g (*2 oz*) butter
salt and freshly ground black pepper

Gently fry the onion and mushrooms in the fat, until soft. Add 25 g (*1 oz*) of the flour and stir over a low heat for 2-3 minutes. Blend in the milk and stir as the liquid comes to the boil and thickens. Season lightly and add the Worcestershire sauce, parsley and crabmeat.

Blend the mashed potatoes with the crabmeat mixture. Chill until firm enough to form into eight round cakes.

Season the remaining flour and use to coat the crab cakes. Brush them with beaten egg, then roll in the breadcrumbs. Heat the oil or butter in a large frying pan and fry the cakes until crisp and brown on both sides.

POTATO BREAD

Makes a 1 kg (2 lb) loaf or 16 rolls

250 g (*8 oz*) strong white flour
250 g (*8 oz*) wholemeal flour
7 g (*¼ oz*) sachet fast-action dried yeast
2 teaspoons salt
125 g (*4 oz*) mashed potato, sieved
250 ml (*8 fl oz*) warm water
milk, to glaze

Mix the flours, yeast and salt in a bowl and rub in the mashed potato. Add the warm water and mix to a soft dough. Turn on to a floured surface and knead for 10 minutes until smooth and elastic.

Shape the dough and place in a greased 1 kg (*2 lb*) loaf tin. Cover with oiled polythene and leave to prove in a warm place for about 45-60 minutes until doubled in bulk. Alternatively, shape the dough into 16 rolls and arrange on greased baking sheets; cover and leave to prove for 25 minutes.

Brush the surface of the loaf or rolls with milk. Bake in a preheated oven, 230°C (*450°F*), Gas Mark 8, for 30-40 minutes until the bread is well risen and sounds hollow when tapped underneath. Turn the loaf out of the tin and cool on a wire rack. Rolls will only require 15 minutes' baking.

ROQUEFORT BREAD

Makes a 500 g (1 lb) loaf

500 g (*1 lb*) strong white flour
2 teaspoons salt
25 g (*1 oz*) butter
7 g (*¼ oz*) sachet fast-action dried yeast
150 ml (*¼ pint*) lukewarm milk
250 g (*8 oz*) cooked potato, sieved
125 g (*4 oz*) Roquefort
or blue cheese, crumbled
beaten egg, to glaze

Sift the flour with the salt into a warmed bowl. Rub in the butter until the mixture resembles fine breadcrumbs. Stir in the yeast. Stir the milk into the sieved potato in a bowl, then work this mixture into the flour to make a soft but not sticky dough. Knead on a floured board for 5 minutes, then knead in the crumbled cheese.

Grease a 500 g (*1 lb*) loaf tin. Shape the dough to fit the tin, or shape into a round cob shape and place on a greased baking sheet. Cover with oiled polythene and leave to rise in a warm place for 30 minutes, or until the loaf has doubled in bulk. Brush with beaten egg and bake in a preheated oven, 200°C (*400°F*), Gas Mark 6, for 15 minutes. Reduce the heat to 180°C (*350°F*), Gas Mark 4, and bake for 15 minutes more. Turn the loaf out of the tin, if using, and leave to cool on a wire rack.

Illustrated opposite

CHOCOLATE PUDDING WITH CHOCOLATE SAUCE

Serves 4

125 g (*4 oz*) butter
125 g (*4 oz*) caster sugar
2 eggs, beaten
25 g (*1 oz*) cocoa powder
1 teaspoon baking powder
125 g (*4 oz*) cooked potato, sieved
50 g (*2 oz*) ground almonds

CHOCOLATE SAUCE:

150 ml (*¼ pint*) single cream
125 g (*4 oz*) plain chocolate,
broken into squares

Cream the butter and caster sugar together in a large mixing bowl until light and fluffy. Gradually beat in the eggs, beating well after each addition.

Sift the cocoa powder and baking powder together and gently fold into the mixture, then fold in the sieved cooked potato and the ground almonds.

Turn the mixture into a greased 1 litre (*1¾ pint*) pudding basin. Cover the basin with a circle of greased greaseproof paper and then with a circle of foil which has been pleated to allow room for the pudding to rise. Secure the paper covering securely with string.

Steam the chocolate pudding on a trivet or upturned saucer in a saucepan half-filled with boiling water for 1½ hours – adding more boiling water to the pan as necessary. When the pudding is cooked, remove the pudding basin from the saucepan and leave to stand for 5 minutes.

Meanwhile, to make the chocolate sauce, bring the single cream to the boil in a small saucepan, then remove from the heat. Add the chocolate pieces, stirring until they have melted and the sauce is smooth.

Turn the pudding out on to a heated dish and serve it immediately, with the hot chocolate sauce poured over.

NECTARINE CHEESE FLAN

Serves 6

75 g (*3 oz*) self-raising flour
25 g (*1 oz*) ground hazelnuts
½ teaspoon mixed spice
50 g (*2 oz*) butter
75 g (*3 oz*) cooked potato, mashed
65 g (*2½ oz*) caster sugar
1 egg, lightly beaten
125 g (*4 oz*) full-fat soft cheese
½ teaspoon vanilla essence
3 nectarines, halved and stoned

Place the flour, ground hazelnuts and mixed spice together in a large bowl. Mix well together then rub in the butter with your fingertips. Stir in the mashed potato and 50 g (*2 oz*) of the caster sugar and knead lightly until the mixture forms a dough.

Lightly grease a 20 cm (*8 inch*) loose-based fluted flan tin and press the dough into the prepared tin with floured fingertips. Press the dough well into the sides and prick well all over with a fork.

Place the case in the centre of a preheated oven, 190°C (*375°F*), Gas Mark 5, and bake for 25-30 minutes until lightly browned. Remove the flan case from the oven and reduce the temperature to 180°C (*350°F*), Gas Mark 4.

Meanwhile, place the beaten egg, soft cheese, vanilla essence and remaining caster sugar in a bowl and mix together.

Place the nectarine halves on a work surface. Using a sharp knife cut each half into 5 mm (*¼ inch*) slices, keeping the slices together.

Arrange five of the nectarine halves around the edge of the cooked flan case and one in the centre of the flan, slightly fanning out the slices. Carefully spoon the soft cheese mixture over the nectarines to cover all of the fruit and the flan base.

Return the flan to the oven and bake for 30-35 minutes until the filling is set and lightly golden. Carefully ease the flan out of the tin and serve warm with cream.

FARMHOUSE FRUIT CAKE

Serves 10-12

175 g (*6 oz*) **soft margarine**
175 g (*6 oz*) **demerara sugar**
125 g (*4 oz*) **mashed potato, sieved**
1 tablespoon **golden syrup**
125 g (*4 oz*) **plain flour**
125 g (*4 oz*) **wholemeal flour**
3 teaspoons **baking powder**
1 teaspoon **mixed spice**
3 **eggs, beaten**
125 g (*4 oz*) **sultanas**
125 g (*4 oz*) **raisins**
50 g (*2 oz*) **almonds, chopped**
50 g (*2 oz*) **glacé cherries, quartered**
demerara sugar, for sprinkling

Place the soft margarine and demerara sugar in a mixing bowl and cream together until pale and fluffy. Beat in the mashed potato and golden syrup.

In a second bowl, blend together the plain and wholemeal flour, the baking powder and the mixed spice. Gradually beat the eggs into the creamed potato mixture, a little at a time, adding some of the flour mixture if necessary to prevent curdling.

Fold in the remainder of the flour to the mixture, together with the sultanas, raisins, chopped almonds and glacé cherries.

Line and grease a 20 cm (*8 inch*) deep cake tin. Spoon the cake mixture into the prepared tin and sprinkle the top with demerara sugar.

Place the cake in the centre of a preheated oven, 150°C (*300°F*), Gas Mark 2, and bake for 2½ hours, or until the cake has risen and is firm to the touch.

Leave the cake in the tin for 5 minutes, then turn out on to a wire rack, remove the lining paper and allow to cool. Serve the fruit cake cut into wedges.

Illustrated opposite

POTATO GINGERBREAD

Makes 12-15 slices

150 g (*5 oz*) plain flour
1 teaspoon baking powder
1 teaspoon mixed spice
1 teaspoon ground ginger
pinch of salt
75 g (*3 oz*) potato, peeled and grated
25 g (*1 oz*) glacé cherries, chopped
50 g (*2 oz*) sultanas
125 g (*4 oz*) golden syrup
50 g (*2 oz*) butter
1 egg, beaten
1 teaspoon bicarbonate of soda
1 tablespoon water

Sift the flour, baking powder, mixed spice, ground ginger and salt into a mixing bowl. Stir in the grated potato, glacé cherries and sultanas and mix well.

Melt the syrup and butter in a small saucepan, allow to cool slightly, then add to the dry ingredients with the egg. Mix the soda with the water and add to the mixture. Beat well.

Spoon the mixture into a greased and lined 23 x 12 cm (*9 x 5 inch*) loaf tin. Bake in a preheated oven, 180°C (*350°F*), Gas Mark 4, for 40 minutes, or until the gingerbread feels firm to the touch. Turn out on to a wire rack to cool.

DATE & NUT TEALOAF

Makes 12-15 slices

250 g (*8 oz*) dates, stoned and roughly chopped
50 g (*2 oz*) walnuts, chopped
25 g (*1 oz*) margarine
1 teaspoon bicarbonate of soda
125 g (*4 oz*) demerara sugar
175 ml (*6 fl oz*) boiling water
1 egg, beaten
250 g (*8 oz*) self-raising flour
75 g (*3 oz*) mashed potato, sieved

Place the chopped dates, walnuts, margarine, bicarbonate of soda and demerara sugar in a bowl. Pour over the boiling water, mix well and allow to cool. Stir in the beaten egg, flour and sieved mashed potato and beat well with a wooden spoon.

Spoon into a greased and lined 23 x 12 cm (*9 x 5 inch*) loaf tin and bake in a preheated oven, 180°C (*350°F*), Gas Mark 4, for 1 hour. Cover the loaf with foil and bake for a further 15-20 minutes until firm.

Turn out and allow to cool on a wire rack. Serve sliced, with butter.

APRICOT & SULTANA SCONES

Makes 12

125 g (*4 oz*) plain flour
3 teaspoons baking powder
½ teaspoon salt
½ teaspoon ground cinnamon
50 g (*2 oz*) butter
125 g (*4 oz*) cooked potato, mashed
25 g (*1 oz*) caster sugar
25 g (*1 oz*) sultanas
25 g (*1 oz*) ready-to-eat dried apricots, chopped
1 egg, lightly beaten

Sift the flour, baking powder, salt and ground cinnamon into a bowl. Rub in the butter and mix in the mashed potato. Stir in the caster sugar, sultanas and dried apricots.

Add about half of the beaten egg and mix lightly to form a soft dough. Turn the dough out on to a floured surface and roll out to about 1.5 cm (¾ *inch*) thick. Cut it into 12 rounds with a 5 cm (*2 inch*) cutter.

Place the rounds on a baking sheet, brush with the remaining egg and bake in a preheated oven, 220°C (*425°F*), Gas Mark 7, for 10-12 minutes until the scones are brown and well risen.

Cook on a wire rack. Serve split and buttered.

RUM TRUFFLES

Makes 20

250 g (*8 oz*) plain chocolate, broken into squares
125 g (*4 oz*) mashed potato
175 g (*6 oz*) icing sugar, sifted
1 tablespoon rum, or a few drops of rum essence
chocolate vermicelli

Melt the chocolate in a heatproof basin over a saucepan of hot water, then gradually beat the chocolate into the mashed potato in a bowl. Cover and allow to stand until cold, then beat in the icing sugar and the rum or rum essence. Refrigerate until firm.

Roll the mixture into balls about the size of a walnut. Dip the balls into the chocolate vermicelli and place in small paper sweet cases. Store in the refrigerator until required – they are ideal served with coffee after dinner.